UNBREAKABLE

UNBREAKABLE

The Journey to Becoming Enough!

Robert J Slade

Published by Game Changer Publishing

Paperback ISBN: 978-1-968250-27-0

Hardcover ISBN: 978-1-968250-28-7

Digital ISBN: 978-1-968250-29-4

GC GAME CHANGER
PUBLISHING
www.GameChangerPublishing.com

ACKNOWLEDGMENTS

First and foremost, I want to give thanks to God and to my parents for giving me life, leading me, guiding me, and doing the best they could for me.

I want to thank my wife for never giving up on me, for being my rock when I was lost, for loving me unconditionally, and for seeing the person I truly can be and am continually working toward becoming. Growing and learning is LIFE.

I want to thank all of my children. I am so grateful for the opportunity to be your father. I am thankful for the lessons and the blessings each of you has brought into my life. Each of you is amazing and will always be enough. Thank you for reminding me that sometimes I need to remind myself that I am enough, too. I'm so proud of each and every one of you, and I am grateful for the grandchildren you have blessed me with.

I want to thank my brothers and sisters for always believing in their big brother—even when I was trying to figure life out and making poor choices. You have never given up on me or on each other. I am grateful to have a large family and to have been taught the value of family unity.

I want to thank everyone who was there when I was at my lowest.

To my therapist—thank you for helping me look within myself and realize that I truly am enough. You helped me see that the past is the past. But in order to leave the pain behind, we must learn to forgive and understand our own feelings. Anger is like drinking poison and expecting the other person to get sick.

I want to thank everyone who chose to buy my book, for whatever reason. I want you to know that you are enough and can accomplish everything you set your mind to. What it takes is believing in yourself first. Know that you are enough. You have value. And to all of you: never, ever give up on yourself. Always move forward, knowing you are enough.

READ THIS FIRST

Just to say thanks for buying and reading my book,
I would like to connect with you!

Scan the QR Code Here:
Always Forward Health Wellness (My Business)

UNBREAKABLE

THE JOURNEY TO BECOMING ENOUGH!

ROBERT J SLADE

PREFACE

There was a time in my life when I believed strength meant silence —when I wore my pain like armor and convinced myself that resilience meant never cracking, never crying, never needing help.

But life has a way of stripping away the surface.

In 2005, I was wounded in combat while serving in the Army in Iraq. The physical injury was one thing—but the invisible wounds ran deeper. I returned home with questions no uniform or title could answer. Who was I now? Was I still whole? Still worthy? Still *enough*?

This book is the journey of what came next.

It's not just about war. It's about the battle we all face: the one between who we were, who we pretend to be, and who we are becoming. I had to confront my own brokenness, my shame, my doubts—and somewhere in the rubble, I found redemption. I found grace. I found *me*.

I've lived many lives—soldier, survivor, husband, father of six, grandfather, health and wellness consultant. I've been humbled more times than I can count. But through it all, I've learned that our worth isn't tied to what we've achieved or what we've lost. It's not something we earn. It's something we reclaim.

Unbreakable: The Journey to Becoming Enough! is more than a title. It's a truth I fought hard to believe—and now, it's a truth I live to share. My hope is that as you walk through these pages, you begin to see your own story reflected here. That you find strength in your scars, power in your voice, and peace in knowing you were never too far gone.

This isn't the end of my story. And it's not the end of yours either.

You are worthy. You are seen. You are *enough*.

Let's walk this journey together.

—RJ Slade

CONTENTS

INTRODUCTION

My name is Robert Slade, though I prefer to go by R.J.

I am a U.S. Army combat veteran. I am a father. I am a husband. I am a grandfather, a brother, a son. But more importantly, I am someone who views the world as a place where I can take what I've learned and give back. What led me to where I am today is told in this book—a story I hope will inspire and remind each of us that we are unique.

This book isn't necessarily for a woman, a man, a boy, or a girl—it's for everyone. I hope that by taking the time to read it, you'll find inspiration in my stories (some of which could probably be turned into a country song!) and discover that you are enough, just as you are.

I hold a master's degree in Public Administration from Purdue. I am a nationally certified health and wellness coach, a certified nutritionist, a certified life coach, a certified health coach, a certified transformation specialist, and a certified personal trainer. All of these certifications—along with the master's in Clinical Nutrition that I've just started—have been part of my journey to better understand how to manage my mental and physical health more effectively. I knew there had to be a better way than what we were being taught. And I hope, as I said, that this book helps lead you down a path of inspiration and supports you in reaching your goals.

Before we begin, I want to take you back to where it all started —my earliest childhood memories.

As children, we view the world through innocent eyes, deeply shaped by the voices and actions of the adults around us. We see our parents as infallible, their words as law, their choices as our roadmap. We don't yet understand that they, too, are on a journey— imperfect, learning, growing—just like we are.

But here's the truth I want to remind you of from the very beginning: **we were never meant to be perfect.**

In this book, I share with you the moments, lessons, and turning points that shaped my path—the choices I made, the detours I took, and the revelations I uncovered along the way. What I discovered in the process is something I hope you'll discover too: **you are enough —just as you are.**

Each chapter is designed not only to tell a story but to spark something in you. Whether it's clarity, healing, courage, or a renewed sense of purpose, I believe you'll find pieces of your own journey reflected in mine.

So come walk this road with me. Let these stories speak to your heart, challenge your perspective, and remind you of the strength, resilience, and greatness already within you.

1

EARLY INFLUENCES ON THE FIELD

I am the oldest of seven children. My mother and father had seven kids in eleven years, and I was born to teenage parents who have now been together for forty-nine years. My story as a young child begins when I was seven years old. Without question, I began to step up and help my mother with my younger brothers. After having my fourth brother, my mother became ill. I started helping her by getting bottles for the babies, vacuuming, and cooking meals for the family—doing many things that most kids today don't have the opportunity to learn through experience. People have told me that I was already a young adult at seven, learning what it meant to be a teammate.

As life transitioned, my young mind began to question things, as any child would. The first time I realized that adults can make mistakes—and that people aren't perfect—was as I got older and became interested in a variety of activities: singing, playing the trombone, and playing sports. But which one would I truly enjoy? My father encouraged me to pursue sports. He coached me in everything from soccer and snow-skiing starting at age five, to football when I turned eight, and into junior high school, as well as in baseball and Little League.

One story from that time stands out—one that shifted how I viewed my father and other adults. As children, we often see adults as protectors, as people who always do the right thing. We don't yet understand that everyone is human and makes mistakes. I want to be clear: I don't hold any anger toward my father for the choices he made then or afterward. But the moment that opened my eyes happened when I was nine years old, struggling to stay in the batter's box during fast-pitch baseball. We had been at the baseball diamond for about an hour, with him pitching to me again and again. As a young boy, I started feeling worn out and bored from repeating the same drill. I didn't yet understand the value of practice. I could tell my father was growing frustrated because I kept stepping out of the batter's box.

Eventually, he told me sternly, "You need to stay in the batter's box. Quit being afraid of the ball. If it's coming at you, move—but you need to stay in there and try to hit it." I got frustrated too, and decided I would stay in the box no matter what. Between our shared frustration, my father threw a pitch with more force than usual. I stayed in the box—and the ball hit my hand. I ended up losing a thumbnail.

That was the first time I truly saw my father as an imperfect adult. He didn't mean to hurt me. He wasn't trying to cause pain. But that moment showed me that even the people we look up to can feel anger and frustration. No one is perfect. We're all here to learn and grow, to question everything, to come into this world with eyes wide open, ready to absorb and hopefully thrive. I've always been grateful to my parents for giving me life, for doing the best they could, and for teaching me the value of family unity, of loving others, of being human, and of seeing the value in everyone. In the end, it's our actions that define our character.

From then on, I began to see my father differently and realized that a lot of what I was doing—as the second man of the house, so to speak—wasn't being appreciated. I was helping my mother, trying to take on responsibilities as a young boy, but it didn't feel like it mattered. I now understand that this came from my father's upbringing and other factors, but as a child, you're just lost. You don't understand why adults act the way they do toward you, or why everything you do doesn't feel like it's enough.

I thought that standing in that batter's box and taking the hit would make my dad proud of me. But even then, it still didn't feel like it was enough. As a young boy, that lack of appreciation was painful—especially when I couldn't share my feelings with my father. My father grew up in an era where boys were expected to be tough: don't cry, don't complain, just be a man and handle life. What was missing was the message that it's okay for boys and girls to have feelings. It's okay to cry when you're sad—it actually heals you and releases the toxic stress stored in your body. I carried that belief—the belief that boys shouldn't cry—for many years, even with my own sons. But eventually, my eyes opened, and I realized that boys need unconditional love from their fathers. It's okay if they cry. It's okay if they feel deeply.

At this point in my story, I was still growing, still learning, still trying to understand that I am enough. It hurt. Growing up in the '80s and '90s, boys were expected to be tough, to suppress their emotions, to just keep pushing. But I can tell you now—that approach creates resentment and other issues in young men. When they're not allowed to express their feelings or receive appreciation, it wounds them.

Yes, it's important to encourage boys to grow and persevere, but at that point in my life, I began to question my father—his intentions, and whether I had value in our home. Even though I was helping my mom clean, doing well in school, playing the sports my father wanted me to play, staying active, and trying to follow the direction I thought he expected of me, it never felt like I was doing it well enough.

That created a sense of shame in me from a young age—a deep-rooted belief that everything I did still wasn't enough. And that shame lingered for a long time. So from all of this, from my experience as a child, here's the best advice I can offer to you, my readers: If you're experiencing an identity crisis, or struggling to confront difficult realities about your family or your roots, here are eight things you need to do:

1. First and foremost, you need to **accept that your past does not define you**. Your family and upbringing may have shaped parts of who you are, but they do not determine your future. You are not bound by the limitations, mistakes, or dysfunctions of those who came before you. You have the power to create your own path.

2. **Seek the truth**, even when it hurts. Facing reality, whether it involves painful family dynamics, generational trauma, or the feeling of not being enough, is difficult. But the truth, no matter how heavy, is the foundation of true freedom. Denial only prolongs suffering. Acknowledge what is, and then decide how you will rise above it. Decide what path you'll take moving forward.

4

3. **Redefine who you are** on your own terms. If you feel lost, start by asking yourself: What values truly matter to me? What kind of person do I want to be? What strengths have I gained from my struggles? What brings me fulfillment? Your identity isn't something you find—it's something you build, one decision at a time.

4. **Distance yourself from toxic influences.** If your family or past environment causes more harm than good, it's okay to set boundaries. You do not owe anyone your peace—especially if their presence drains you or diminishes your light. Protect your growth at all costs.

5. **Embrace both strength and vulnerability.** Strength isn't about pretending to have it all figured out. It's about owning your struggles and using them as fuel for growth. Allow yourself to grieve, to question, and to heal. There is no shame in seeking guidance—from a mentor, a counselor, or a trusted friend.

6. **Forgive**, not for them, but for you. Forgiveness doesn't mean excusing or forgetting. It means freeing yourself from the weight of resentment so you can move forward unburdened. Let go of the pain so you can hold on to your peace.

7. **Find your true tribe**. If your roots don't feel like home, plant new ones. Surround yourself with people who uplift you, who understand you, who accept you. Family isn't always blood—it's the people who show up for you, support you, and walk beside you on your journey.

8. **Keep moving forward**, no matter how uncertain the path. You don't need all the answers right now. Just take the

next step. Growth happens in uncertainty, and strength is built through the process of overcoming.

And my final thought: You are not broken. You are becoming. The struggles you face now are shaping you into someone with wisdom, resilience, and depth. Stand tall in your truth, and never let the weight of your past keep you from rising into your future.

Chapter 1 Challenge: The Gratitude Challenge

Every day for one week, write down three things you're grateful for. Reflect on how this shift in mindset changes your energy and perspective.

_____

_____

_____

_____

2

QUESTIONING FAITH AND VALUES

As a young boy going through puberty, I found many things confusing—just as most people do, whether you're a boy or a girl. Your hormones are all over the place, your emotions are intense, and you constantly wonder what's wrong with you. One thing I did know: I was struggling. I didn't understand why I felt out of balance, why I was experiencing depression, why I didn't feel peace in my religion. I was confused about why so many adults would tell me to live one way, and then act in completely different ways themselves. That contradiction was hard to process as a young person—especially when I'd been raised within a specific religion, where values were taught as absolute, but the reality often revealed hypocrisy. What's worse was when those values became a source of shame rather than support.

I was raised in the LDS Church—also known as Latter-day Saints or Mormons. It was the only religion I knew. Like most people, I was born into the faith my parents practiced. And to be clear, I don't believe there's anything wrong with being spiritual or following Christianity or any other faith. But the problems I began questioning as a boy had to do with what I was observing. I saw value in helping my mother and doing the right thing, but I started to notice that much of what I was being taught in church didn't line up with what I believed was the core purpose: learning about God. Instead, the focus often felt centered around the church's specific prophet. And yet, in the Bible, it says not to worship false prophets or specific buildings. That deeply conflicted with what I was being told in LDS teachings—especially when surrounded by temples and structures that felt more like monuments to the religion than pathways to God.

So, around the age of 14, I started questioning my faith, my values, and what I was being taught. As I pulled away from church attendance, I started noticing that friends I had grown up with were no longer allowed to play with me—just because I didn't go to church. And that kind of social rejection stings, especially during adolescence. You're trying to find yourself, and all around you are people judging you for not following a specific path, even though you're not doing anything wrong.

Every teenager on this planet deserves the chance to find themselves and their own path. What they need most are supportive, loving adults. That's all I wanted as a young adult—support while I asked hard questions about my faith. I took the more difficult path because, for me, the facts and experiences simply didn't align with what I was being taught. Internally, something didn't sit right, and I felt compelled to follow what felt true to me. I sensed that a veil had been placed over my eyes, and I knew I had to lift it to discover who I truly was—without guilt for every choice I made or fear that I was a sinner or a disappointment. I wasn't questioning whether God existed. I never stopped believing in Him. I was questioning the religion I had been raised in—the specific doctrines and teachings that, even now, still don't align with my truth.

When people ask, I tell them I'm spiritual. I have a relationship with Jesus—but Jesus is not my religion. I try to walk in His path by loving myself and knowing that I am enough. I try to live with forgiveness, knowing that forgiveness doesn't require an apology, nor does it mean inviting toxicity back into my life. I strive not to judge the person—but instead, to make decisions based on their actions.

I even tried to approach it respectfully when I told my parents that I wanted to explore other religions and faiths—because, to be honest, I just didn't feel God in the religion I was raised in. I told them I wanted to be like their founder and seek out truth in other religions, to see if I could find God elsewhere. My parents have always been supportive, but I could tell my father wasn't happy about it. That only pushed me further away. I began to feel outcast by my community and neighborhood simply because I didn't go to church.

I started hanging out with kids whose parents weren't as religious or didn't go to church at all. I got into smoking, drinking, and causing mischief—things that didn't align with who I really was inside. I've always been someone who wants to help others, someone who genuinely wants to understand why things are the way they are. Regardless of the reasons, I've always had this drive to grow and learn. Whether my choices were good or bad, I owned them, and I put all my energy into the path I had chosen.

Maybe that drive came from being a boy who, as I talked about in Chapter 1, took on a lot of responsibility helping my mother. It taught me so much—even if, at the time, I didn't always appreciate it or see the value in it. But when you're trying to find your balance and your roots, and the very people who should be supporting you reject you for asking questions and choosing a different path, it creates a whole new struggle—especially for a teenager. On top of that, I lost most of my friends. That made me ask myself: *Is it better to go along with something you're questioning—just to fit in and have friends—or is it better to walk away and be true to yourself?* I chose the harder path.

I chose to be the one the neighborhood rejected. I became the kid parents blamed when their children got caught smoking or doing something wrong. I was the scapegoat. Even my own father blamed me for a long time when my little brother started smoking cigarettes at a young age.

But in the end, everyone makes their own choices—just like we do as young adults. So never let others dictate your faith, your questions, or your beliefs. If you're searching for deeper answers, don't worry about the people who shun you or walk away.

Because in the end, once you find those answers, it's going to be worth it. So, the best advice I can give to my readers is this:

1. **Embrace the process without fear.** Doubt is not the enemy of faith—it's a tool that refines it. Questioning what you've always believed doesn't mean you're lost. It means you're searching for a deeper, more personal truth.

2. **Identify the root of your doubt.** Ask yourself: *Am I questioning my beliefs because of pain, personal experiences, loss, or disappointment? Have I inherited values without truly understanding them? Do I feel pressured to conform to beliefs that no longer align with who I am?* Understanding *why* you're questioning helps you find answers that resonate with your soul.

3. **Seek truth, not just comfort.** It's tempting to ignore your doubts to feel safe. But real peace only comes from facing those doubts head-on. Read, study, and engage in honest conversations with people who challenge and expand your perspective.

4. **Don't let others dictate your faith or values.** You're the one walking your path. You're the one who has to live with the choices you make. Choose the path that aligns with your truth—not someone else's expectations. Your beliefs should be your own—not just something inherited from your family, culture, or society. It's okay if your journey doesn't look like anyone else's.

5. **Separate faith from people.** If your doubts stem from hypocrisy, judgment, or harm caused by religious or moral institutions, remember that people are flawed. Don't let the failures of others define your relationship with your faith or values.

6. **Allow yourself time and space.** You don't have to figure everything out overnight. Give yourself grace and allow time to explore, reflect, and evolve—without guilt or pressure.

7. **Stay grounded in integrity.** Even when you're questioning faith, hold on to your core values— kindness, honesty, and respect. Your moral compass doesn't have to disappear just because your beliefs are shifting.

8. **Find a supportive community.** Surround yourself with people who respect your journey rather than judge it. Seek mentors, spiritual leaders, or friends who offer wisdom without imposing their own agendas.

9. **Accept the growth.** Understand that growth can be uncomfortable. Letting go of old beliefs can feel like losing a part of yourself—but remember, growth often requires shedding what no longer serves you to make space for what does. Sometimes, you simply need to empty the cup and start over—and that's okay.

10. **Define your own truth.** At the end of the day, your faith and values should bring you peace, strength, and purpose. No one else can dictate what that looks like for you.

And one final thought: Questioning doesn't mean you're lost. It means you're searching for something real. And that's a journey worth taking. Trust yourself. Embrace the uncertainty. And know that, in time, clarity will come.

Chapter 2 Challenge: The Mind-Body Challenge

Commit to moving your body intentionally every day for ten to thirty minutes. This could be stretching, yoga, walking, strength training—whatever feels good to you. The goal is to reconnect with your body and feel present in your movement. I'm not here to tell anyone which path to take—only to encourage you to follow the one that feels right for you, whether it's easy or difficult.

3

TURBULENCE IN JUNIOR HIGH

Like any teenager—as we touched on in Chapter 2—we go through hormonal changes, identity struggles, and a deep desire to find our place in the world. Every single one of us goes through growth spurts and physical changes during adolescence. Whether you're active or not, whether you gain a little weight or fill out or stay skinny, none of it should define your worth. You need to remember to love yourself. And honestly, the American diet—full of quick, processed, and ultra-processed foods—plays a major role in children's growth and weight. No one expected that synthetic chemicals and preservatives would be approved for use in our food, but here we are.

Like many others, I struggled with self-image during junior high. I was seen as the chubby skateboarder. But when I played football, that same size was praised—because I could run people over when I had the ball, or block effectively for teammates. Still, even with that, all I really wanted was to feel like I belonged—to feel connected with my peers and accepted by those around me.

Additionally, in the '80s and '90s, when I was growing up, there were distinct cliques. You were either a skater, a rocker, a gang member, a bowhead, a valley girl, a jock, or a preppy. These labels were mostly based on clothing styles, hobbies, or involvement in sports. But even then, I didn't really align with any one category. I played football and baseball. I also skateboarded. I had friends from every ethnic background and every clique. I've always judged people based on their actions—not by the clothes they wear, their social status, or the color of their skin. We are so much more than the surface-level norms that society wants us to believe. Unfortunately, as we grow up, the beliefs and behaviors we learn from adults and peers—who themselves were shaped by their upbringing—are often reflected in how we treat others.

Just because I skateboarded, a group of gang members decided to target me. I'm not going to give value to the gang's name or the ethnic backgrounds of those involved—because that's not the point. These gang members would make darts out of pencil erasers and push pins, load them into hollow pen tubes, and shoot them at students walking down the hallway. It was bullying. It was intimidation. It was meant to make them look like a threat—someone others shouldn't mess with.

One incident stands out. I skateboarded to school every day— about a mile—and by the time I got to junior high, I was mentally prepared to face threats in the hallway. These same gang members had been harassing me regularly. They mocked me for being a skateboarder, made fun of my long hair—which, at the time, was styled in a "waver" look, combed to one side. They called me names: "fat boy," "doughboy," "chubby," "skater," "waver." The insults were constant.

One morning, as I was walking down the hallway, I got shot in the back with a dart. And, true to who I am—the kind of person who challenges everything, whether it's religion, facts, or authority —I wasn't going to run. I've always been a fighter, not a runner. So, I turned around and gave those gang members a piece of my mind. Things escalated quickly—they got aggressive with me, and I ended up hitting one of them with my skateboard as he came at me. I was taken to the office and my mother was called.

Thankfully, I didn't get in trouble—it was clearly self-defense. Still, it scared my mother. She thought it would be best to move me in with her parents and transfer me to a new junior high school. At the time, I didn't understand why. I wasn't afraid of those gang members—I had stood my ground.

Sure, I got into trouble, but I didn't get kicked out of school because they were the aggressors, and I was defending myself. I had my skateboard in my hand, and I used it in self-defense. It was a reaction to being shot in the back with darts and facing three gang members charging at me. It didn't matter that I was only thirteen years old—I reacted the way any human would react to protect themselves from harm. In the end, we all try to preserve our safety. But even so, my mom made the decision to move me to a new school and have me live with my grandparents.

That meant starting over completely—new school, new community, and the challenge of trying to find a new group to fit in with. I didn't play football with the kids there, so I didn't connect with the jocks. I had no friends yet, and I didn't know who belonged to what clique. I hoped I could at least find some skaters to befriend. At the same time, I was already making poor choices. I had started smoking cigarettes, using cannabis, and doing other things I'm not proud of.

So in the end, standing up for myself only seemed to push me further into isolation. First, I had been outcast by my local friends because I chose not to go to church. And now, I was being taken away from my entire neighborhood. Luckily, my grandparents lived only about two miles from my parents' house. But I still had to walk, skateboard, or ride a bike back over to the old neighborhood just to hang out with the few friends I still had. Even then, I often felt deeply alone and lost—through junior high and even into my sophomore year of high school.

The best lessons I can share from that time—and my advice for readers—starts with this:

1. **Understand your hormonal changes.** It's not just you. Hormones shift constantly during your teen years. They affect your mood, energy, and emotions. Some days you'll feel on top of the world. Other days, everything will feel frustrating, sad, or pointless. That's normal—and it's okay. This is all part of growing, learning, and evolving.

2. **Support your body.** Help yourself through these times by eating nutrient-dense foods: whole grains, proteins, healthy fats, and fiber. These help keep your blood sugar stable and reduce mood swings. Get moving—exercise releases feel-good hormones that help balance your emotions. Even a short walk or a few pushups can make a real difference.

3. **Prioritize your sleep.** Lack of sleep makes hormonal imbalance worse. Aim for eight to ten hours a night. I know spending time with your friends seems like the most important thing in the world, but trust me, getting enough rest will improve your mood, personality, and overall mental health.

4. **Talk about it.** Don't keep it all inside. You are *not* alone. Talk to someone you trust—a parent, a coach, a teacher, or a friend who understands. Reaching out is not weakness. It's strength. It's better to talk about what you're going through than to hold it in and carry it all by yourself.

One area where this is of special relevance is in dealing with bullies.

Dealing with Bullies

Bullying is painful, but it doesn't define your worth. People who bully often act out of their own insecurities—but that doesn't make it right. Bullies tend to project their inner struggles onto others. In fact, we all do that sometimes—we project our internal emotions onto the world around us. But still, that doesn't justify bullying. So, what can you do?

Stay confident—even if you don't feel it. Bullies thrive on reactions. If you act unbothered, you take away their power.

Use humor. A well-placed joke or calm response can catch them off guard. For example, if someone says, "You're weird," try replying with, "Thanks! I prefer to be unique."

Find your tribe. Surround yourself with friends who lift you up. Even one true friend can make all the difference. Pay attention to those who are there for both your laughter and your tears.

Tell someone you trust. A teacher, parent, or counselor can help. Asking for support is not weakness—it's a sign of strength.

Chapter 3 Challenge: A Daily Act of Kindness

Do one kind thing for someone each day—whether it's a compliment, an act of service, or simply a genuine smile. Notice how kindness shifts your mood. Pay attention to how it makes you feel inside. Kindness has a way of blocking out the negative and opening space for joy and connection.

You just need to remember this: **You are not here by mistake. You are enough.** Truly. That simple truth is what carried me through everything I endured. Sure, I had some good friends, but they could only do so much. At that age, I couldn't drive or get around easily, and I often had to face things on my own. But reminding myself—again and again—that I was enough, just by being who I was, kept me going. You are here on this planet for a reason. And that reason matters.

4

SEEKING

Redemption Through Scouting

As all this turbulence unfolded in my life—getting moved to live with my grandparents and, for a short time, with my uncle (which only lasted a couple of months before I was back with my grandparents)—my mom was trying everything she could to protect me. I think, in her way, she was trying to place me where I could be around good mentors and influences. At the time, I didn't really see it that way, but looking back, I understand.

One thing I did know for sure was that I wanted my parents to be proud of me. All children want that. From a young age, making our parents happy is something many of us deeply desire. We thrive on knowing they're proud. So when my mom came to me with a suggestion—knowing I was nearing sixteen and close to being eligible for a driver's license—she encouraged me, perhaps without even realizing the full impact it would have, to pursue my Eagle Scout rank. It was a way to help me stay focused and avoid falling deeper into the negativity and idle time that had surrounded me. She told me that if I earned my Eagle Scout, she would let me get my driver's license.

That was a huge incentive for me. If I still had to live with my grandparents and go to a different high school the following year, having a license would give me the freedom to see my friends and gain a sense of independence.

I saw Boy Scouting not only as a path to a great reward but also as an outlet—something that would give me structure and purpose. I worked hard. I earned my Arrow of Light in Cub Scouting, advanced through the ranks, and eventually reached Eagle Scout. To earn the Eagle Scout award, you have to complete a community service project—something that benefits others. I chose to support the Utah School for Special Needs near Provo, where individuals with special needs live and are supported, often coming from families facing financial hardship.

For my project, I collected and donated clothes, shoes, and other essentials. I coordinated donations and made sure they reached those in need. During this time, I was also helping my mom with her own work. She was a special needs educator and later worked for the State Board of Education, overseeing special education and 504 plans. Helping her in those classrooms gave me a better understanding of individuals with special needs, and I felt compelled to give back. That experience taught me to see the value in every person—especially those society often misunderstands or overlooks. It helped remove fear and judgment.

As young people, we sometimes make fun of those who are different. But why? Is it because we're afraid? Because we don't understand them? What does "normal" really mean? These are questions we should always ask ourselves.

Through scouting, I learned the power of teamwork, the value of commitment, and what I could achieve if I really applied myself. It reminded me that I *am enough*. That no matter the pressure or chaos around me, if I could focus on something meaningful, something I believed in, I could thrive. For me, earning my Eagle Scout was one of those defining achievements. And it paid off. I earned it by the time I turned sixteen—and I made my mother proud. And I know my mom understood that if she didn't give me that challenge—if I didn't earn my Eagle Scout by the time I turned sixteen—I probably never would. So I'm very grateful she came up with that goal for me.

Key learnings from this experience: Scouting provided a structure that challenged me through the pursuit of merit badges and other awards. It taught me the importance of finding something you're interested in—something that encourages personal growth through effort and perseverance. When you focus your energy on positive, meaningful goals, you reduce the time you might otherwise spend making poor choices or engaging in negative self-talk.

Learning useful skills doesn't just create "value" in the abstract —it equips you with tools you can carry into your future. Those tools may one day translate into skills you can use to earn a living. But more importantly, they help build your confidence and resilience. You have to believe in yourself. You have to know you're strong enough to keep pushing forward and to accomplish the things you set out to do. Because if you're not willing to push, and you're not willing to keep going, then you're not going to find success. Dreams will remain dreams unless you act. They won't become reality on their own.

Your strength lies within you. If there's something you deeply believe in—something you're truly passionate about—listen to that inner voice that's nudging you in a good direction. So often, that inner voice is guiding us toward the right path. And when we ignore it, we usually find ourselves in trouble. Even in small things —like that moment when a voice inside says, *Don't stick your hand in the can, you'll cut yourself,* and you think, *I've done this a thousand times.* What happens? You cut your finger. That's life reminding us: **trust your instincts.** Believe in yourself. Trust that inner voice.

At the end of the day, no one else can do that for you. You need to have faith in yourself and in what you know is right for *you*—for your life, your growth, your future. That's really the most important thing I can share with you, the reader: **You have to believe in yourself.** There's no one else on this planet who can do it for you.

And know this: you are unique. You are the manifestation of a one-in-four-trillion chance just by existing. The very fact that your soul is here means you have purpose. Scouting gave me that sense of purpose. Earning merit badges, seeing the smile on my mother's face, feeling like I was slowly doing things that made people proud —those moments mattered. Volunteering, living by the principles of being a good Scout, those values stayed with me. And along the way, I learned practical skills—knot tying, how to shoot a rifle, how to serve selflessly, and how to always be prepared.

These weren't just activities—they were confidence builders. They made me excited to keep learning more and more. Scouting, in many ways, helped shape who I became.

Me at age twelve, far left, hiding my face from a photo at a scouting event.

Chapter 4 Challenge: The Morning Power Routine

For this chapter's challenge, I'd like to introduce the *Morning Power Routine*. For the next seven days, I encourage you to begin each morning with: **five minutes of gentle stretching, ten minutes of deep breathing, and a personal affirmation.**

This affirmation could be something simple, like looking into the mirror and saying: "I am enough. I have value." Or maybe: "Today is going to be an amazing day." Even just waking up and feeling grateful for another day of life can be powerful. Try this routine for seven days straight. Then take a moment to reflect: How do you feel? Has your mindset shifted? Do you feel more centered, more positive, more alive? (I've provided some note lines for you).

Small habits like this can make a big difference in how we show up each day.

_____

_____

_____

_____

5

THE CROSSROADS OF GANG INFLUENCE AND YOUTH CORRECTIONS

Once I got my driver's license, I started working more regularly for my dad, who owned a couple of pizza parlors: Paradise Pizza. I really enjoyed working there, and it became a kind of hangout spot for some of my friends and me during high school. It was one of the jobs I truly enjoyed. I got to deliver pizzas, make pizzas, and learn a lot of different skills.

I had actually started working there when I was just fourteen years old. I didn't *have* to work—I chose to. I wanted to earn enough money to buy myself a skateboard and some shoes. Growing up in a large family of seven children, my parents couldn't always afford to buy us new clothes or extra pairs of shoes during the year. I grew up in an era when you had school clothes and play clothes—and if you wore out your play shoes or good shoes, you might end up duct-taping the soles. That was just life. Sure, we didn't have much, but with my dad owning a pizza parlor, at least we had plenty of free pizza.

As time went on, my friends and I continued to hang out there. But in the late '80s and early '90s, gang culture was becoming more and more influential—especially through pop culture, rap music, and movies. I'm not saying the music *made* us do anything, but back then, movies like *Boyz n the Hood* were hitting theaters, and they often glamorized gang life. To a young kid trying to find his identity, it could seem like those gang members had power, respect, and money. That kind of image was tempting. I've always been into rap music. I still listen to old-school tracks to this day. But the lyrics don't influence me the way they did back then. At that age, they really shaped how I saw the world.

One night, something happened behind my dad's pizza parlor that really stuck with me. Our work shirts were dark blue, and they had a palm tree logo in the center with the words "Paradise Pizza" in a circle around it. That night, my friends and I were out back behind the shop. We were smoking cigarettes—we were underage, but we still did it. I had become addicted to cigarettes, and by then, there was no stopping me. Like many teens, I thought smoking made me feel older, more grown-up—even if it wasn't good for my health.

While we were out back smoking, a car rolled up. Inside were guys wearing red bandanas. One of them stuck a shotgun out the window. We panicked. The back door to the pizza parlor was shut, and none of us wanted to turn our backs to run. Instinct kicked in. All we could do was scatter. After that happened, my friends and I ran and hid under a stairwell in an apartment complex until my dad found us. I guess my grandpa had seen us run off and noticed the car speeding away. He tried to follow us, and thankfully, both he and my dad—who worked together at the pizza parlor—came and found us. My grandfather was a great influence in my life, and I'm grateful they both showed up.

But after that incident, my friends and I started saying, "You know what? If we're going to keep getting picked on by people wearing red bandanas"— "Bloods," as they called themselves in gang culture—"we need to do something." Looking back now, it feels ridiculous that anyone would hurt or threaten someone else over a color, a block, or a neighborhood they didn't even *own*. But that's how we felt then. So we decided it was in our best interest to start a gang of our own. We already had some familiarity with how gang life worked. A few of us had cousins in California who were in gangs. We knew that to be accepted—or "jumped in"—you had to get beat up by the other members. So six of us created our own gang. I'm not going to waste time naming it or going into details, because I'm not here to glorify that life. But the gang grew quickly.

Friends we knew from school and the neighborhood started joining. And before long, it led to more serious things—dealing marijuana and even being involved in drive-by shootings. I didn't personally pull the trigger or take part in the shootings, but I was present at houses when they happened. I was involved by association. One time, I had one of my little brothers with me. There was talk of a possible drive-by coming down a specific street. We were at the house of a close friend of mine—someone who's no longer with us, though he didn't die from anything gang-related, but later in life due to health issues. I don't know how my mom found out where we were, but somehow she did. She showed up—completely unafraid of the risk—and took my little brother home. About fifteen or twenty minutes later, the rival gang drove by and shot up the house we were in.

At the time, I didn't think much of it. Yeah, it was scary, but adrenaline kicks in and kind of numbs the fear. Still, something didn't sit right with me. I didn't feel good about it—not about holding guns, not about shooting at other people. I started to question everything. Why were we fighting people just because they wore red bandanas? Why did that mean we had to hate them? Why did we have to divide ourselves by colors? Why could I be friends with some people, but not others, just based on what they wore?

As the gang activity escalated and the drive-bys became more frequent, one night we were driving through a neighborhood in Kearns. I had several friends in the car, and yes, we had a loaded gun with us—just in case a rival gang tried something. And sure enough, we got shot at. As soon as I heard the shots, I hit the gas and sped out of there. We were trying to get back to one of my friends' houses, get out of the neighborhood, and stay alive. At the time, we had no idea who was shooting at us—or how close we came to real disaster. Just as we were driving past a house in the neighborhood, shots started being fired at my car. Luckily, a bullet ricocheted off one of the doors—if it hadn't, it would've hit one of my friends.

As we continued driving home, a lowrider pickup truck began following us. We thought it was a rival gang. And so, for the first— and only—time in my life, I made the decision to lead them down a back street. We genuinely feared we were about to get shot. While still driving, I took the firearm from my friend, leaned out the window, and fired a shot toward the truck, hoping to scare them into backing off. What none of us in the car knew was that the truck wasn't a rival gang. After I fired and handed the gun to someone in the backseat, one of my friends (I still don't know who) fired additional shots.

I know this might sound like something out of a Hollywood movie, but it was real life. And looking back, it was stupid—reckless and dangerous. As I sped off and made it back onto the main road, I suddenly saw flashing red and blue lights behind me—more than I'd ever seen in my life. There were roadblocks ahead. The street was filled with patrol cars. We later found out that we were being followed by the gang task force—undercover police officers dressed like gang members.

And here's the sad part: looking back, it's very possible we could've been cleared of the charges. Not that I'm justifying shooting out the window—because that's never the right thing to do unless your life is *truly* in danger—but in hindsight, we were caught in a kind of entrapment. Those officers never identified themselves. They were wearing red bandanas and driving a red truck—completely unmarked. We had no way of knowing they were police.

And the one thing I believe truly saved our lives that night? My father and grandfather. Right before that incident happened, they were locking up my dad's pizza parlor. And my grandfather turned to my dad and said, "We need to kneel down and pray. Something bad is going to happen tonight." To this day, I believe I had a guardian angel watching over me. The undercover officers had forgotten to remove their firearms from the locked storage box in the back of their vehicle—so they couldn't return fire. That moment saved all of our lives.

Because, let's be honest—a bunch of sixteen- and seventeen-year-olds with an illegal firearm had no idea what they were doing. Even when I fired, I didn't aim at the truck. I aimed up. I was trying to fire a warning shot. Inside, even though I was scared, my moral compass told me it wasn't right to shoot at someone. They were probably 300–400 yards away—far too far for a pistol to be effective, anyway. But in that moment of panic, surrounded by peer pressure and fear, I made a decision. It wasn't the right one—but it changed my life.

Thankfully, because of the family I came from—my parents were good, religious people—and the fact that I had no prior criminal record, I was given a chance. One of my friend's mothers worked for the Salt Lake County Sheriff's Department. She put in a good word for me, and as a result, I wasn't charged as an adult. Instead, I received a misdemeanor aggravated assault charge, and several other charges were dropped. I was incredibly fortunate. I was placed in a ninety-day program—*Observation and Assessment*—to determine whether I posed a risk to society or could be rehabilitated into a productive adult. And I'm proud to say that I proved that I could. I was able to come out of that experience, walk away from the gang life, and graduate high school with a 4.0 GPA.

The hard part was figuring out where I fit after that. I started spending more time with friends who were more like hippies, I guess you could say—the kind of guys who liked to smoke weed or use psychedelics. But they were mellow, chill, and never interested in fighting or stirring up trouble. Sure, they worked and handled their responsibilities, but in the evenings, they enjoyed unwinding with a little cannabis or occasional psychedelics. There was no stress when I was around those friends.

But even after getting out of juvenile detention, there was pressure to go back—to return to gang life. People would say, "Let's go do this" or "Let's handle that." But I never wanted to sit in a six-by-ten cell again. I never wanted to be told when I could eat or carry the shame and self-hate I felt after that night. So I chose to walk away. Even though that meant risking what, in gang life, is called being *courted out*—getting jumped out. I didn't care. I walked away anyway. And the sad part is, more than thirty years later, there are still people who want to beat me up for leaving. But that didn't change my mind then, and it wouldn't change my mind now. No matter how I look at it, I know I made the right choice.

The best advice I can give you at any crossroads in your life is this: Understand why you're at that crossroads. For me, the gang promised brotherhood, protection, and status. For some people, it's a response to an unstable home life. In my case, I had good parents and a good family. But our house was chaotic—nine people in a four-bedroom home with one working bathroom. And since I was a young boy, I had spent most of my life serving others in that household.

But I didn't always get the "attaboys" I needed. I didn't often hear my father say, "Good job," or "You're doing great, son." Still, I don't blame him.

What kept me going was knowing—deep down—that I was enough. I learned that being told by others that you matter doesn't define you. What matters is that you believe in yourself. That you know, *I am enough.* It's always a gift when someone else reminds you of that truth, but you can't depend on it. You have to believe it first.

Loyalty comes at a price, especially in the gang world. That life brings violence, legal trouble, and a future controlled by someone else. If you're in youth corrections or feeling trapped in a toxic situation, you might feel like your life is already out of your hands. But here's the truth: Your past does not define you. Ask yourself: *Where is this path really taking me? Do I want to live a life where I'm always looking over my shoulder? Who benefits from my choices—me, or someone using me? What kind of future do I want?* You deserve more than being another statistic. But no one is going to hand you a better future. You have to fight for it. And you do that by believing in yourself and knowing that you are enough.

Second, real strength comes from walking away. Leaving a gang —or breaking any toxic cycle—isn't weakness. It takes real courage. It's much harder to walk away and reclaim your life than it is to stay in what's familiar. You give up security, connection, and your identity in that world. But walking away means choosing a path where *you* are in control—not someone else. It's not easy. But neither is sitting in a cell, losing friends to violence, or watching your family suffer because of your choices.

The following are some steps you can follow to break free from all of this:

1. **Start with one decision at a time.** You don't have to change overnight—but every right choice moves you one step closer to a better life.

2. **Distance yourself from toxic influences.** The people you spend time with will either push you forward or pull you backward. Ask yourself: *Are my friends keeping my head just above water, or are they helping lift me out of it?* Choose your circle wisely.

3. **Find a mentor.** This could be a coach, teacher, community leader, or someone who's been in your shoes—someone who can help guide you forward. For me, I had a very influential probation officer at that time. She said a lot of things that stuck with me. And of course, my mother— her unconditional love and constant support—was one of

my greatest mentors. It took me a long time to forgive myself. But listening to them and choosing better friends was one of the best decisions I ever made.

4. **Channel your energy into something positive.** Sports, art, music, business, fitness—whatever it is, find a passion that builds you up instead of breaking you down. Find something that aligns with who you are—something that brings peace, purpose, and pride. Something that makes you feel like you are *enough*.

5. **Own your story and use it to inspire others.** That's what I'm doing with you now. Your struggles, your mistakes, and your hardships can be the very thing that helps someone else change. One day, *you* could be the reason a young person chooses the right path instead of the wrong one. Use your experience for good. Speak to younger kids about making better choices. Get involved in programs that support at-risk youth. Show your family and your community that real change is possible.

Build a future where your past is just one chapter in your life's story—not the whole book. Choose the long-term win over the short-term hustle. Fast money, street respect, and temporary power always come at a cost—jail, death, or a lifetime of regret. The real win is building something lasting. A legal hustle that creates a stable, fulfilling life—whether it's a business, a career, or a job you can grow in.

And a final thought for this chapter: Take a serious look at where your choices are taking you. Are they making life harder—or helping it get better? Yes, some challenges are tough. But true growth comes from doing the hard work, taking ownership, and learning to stop blaming others. Look within and say: *I made these choices. If I want to change my path, then I have to change my direction.* That may mean walking away from friends. It may mean letting go of certain habits. But in the end, to find your own peace, you must find what truly aligns with *you*.

Ask yourself: *What do I need to heal? What makes me feel fulfilled? What makes me feel like I am enough?* Because if you don't believe you're enough—if you don't think you can accomplish something—you'll keep blaming others and stay stuck.

So remember:

- Look within.
- You are enough.
- Your reputation should be based on the skills you bring, the leadership you show, and the respect you earn—not on fear or violence.
- Fear creates nothing lasting.
- Respect builds everything.
- Create a future where *you* control your destiny.

It's not going to be easy, but neither is the alternative.

Chapter 5 Challenge: The No-Excuse Challenge

For one week, remove the phrase "I can't" from your vocabulary. Replace it with: "I haven't learned that yet. I can figure it out."

Tackle one thing you've been procrastinating on—no matter how small. At the end of the week, take a moment to reflect: How did it feel to push through the excuse? What did you learn about yourself? (I've added note lines for you to use.)

_____

_____

_____

_____

6

TRANSFORMATION IN THE MILITARY

As we read and learned in Chapter 5, I was struggling with gangs. I was trying to make decisions, move on, and figure out what an eighteen-year-old guy was supposed to do.

Because in that day and age, at eighteen, you were expected to move out, have your own place, find a job, start a career—those kinds of things. Of course, my father wanted me to work for him or go into construction or do other things, but that really wasn't my path.

So for a short time, I decided to follow my cousins and move to San Antonio, Texas. I lived there for three months, and it ended up being a bad cycle—being around older people who drank way too much. I was an apprentice learning how to install windows, but my job laid me off because they didn't have work for me. An opportunity came up for me to move to Las Vegas, where my great-uncle lived. He was handicapped and had special needs. I was supposed to go live with him in his mobile home park and help care for him, but that ended up being too much of a struggle at eighteen years old, living in Las Vegas.

At the time, I had a great friend who had followed me to San Antonio, then to Las Vegas, and later back to Salt Lake City. Then I moved to St. George, Utah, for a short time. All of this happened within one year. So I was all over the place. Eventually, I moved back to Salt Lake City, where I realized that if I kept surrounding myself with the same influences—the same peers, the same types of people—I was just going to keep repeating the same mistakes. Whether it was in Texas, St. George, or Las Vegas, I kept finding the same kind of crowd, people who weren't going to help me move forward. They were content with staying still—no progress, no direction.

Ultimately, I started making the same bad decisions, selling weed and stuff like that. I became aware that I was being watched by a drug task force from the police department. That realization immediately made me stop and think, *You know what? I'm never going back to jail.* I had learned my lesson from the stupid things I did as a gang member.

Me during my first deployment (left); my first official NCO photo from when I became a sergeant (right).

I decided to join the Army. Two weeks later, I was on a plane to Fort Knox, Kentucky, to begin training. That was a whole new experience—going from complete chaos and not knowing what life was about to arriving somewhere with structure and purpose. What led me to decide to join the military, as I mentioned, was the fact that I had been selling marijuana, mushrooms, and other stuff. I was a young kid experimenting with psychedelics and living like tomorrow would never come—as many young adults do. We often lack direction at that age. But I was lucky—blessed—because one of my friend's mothers, who worked for the county sheriff's office (the same office the drug task force belonged to), saw me at my parents' house one day and said, "Hey, just so you know, the county sheriff's task force has their eye on you."

That immediately raised red flags for me. On top of that, it brought a sense of shame—knowing that a woman who had been like a second mother to me growing up was now warning me. To this day, I still talk about how she used to make us nacho cheese

Doritos and how we'd hang out watching MTV in the basement. She'd bake cookies, too. She was the kind of mom who made you feel at home.

My own mom was great, but with seven brothers, things were always hectic. My friend, on the other hand, was the youngest in his family and basically the only one still living at home—his older siblings had already moved out. So we'd hang out at his house all the time, with his mom bringing us fresh-baked cookies, nachos—everything. She really was like a second mother to me.

My first visit home since joining in 1996 (left); Jungle Terrain training, 2001 (right).

So when that warning came from her, it stopped me in my tracks. I realized I was heading right back down the path to jail. I had tried moving to get away from it all, but I always ended up finding the same people, the same influences, getting sucked back into the same mess I swore I'd leave behind. That's when I knew—it was time to enlist in the military.

When I made that decision, one of my brothers and one of my friends were planning to join with me. Because I was an Eagle Scout, I was able to enlist as a Private Second Class. I probably could have gotten a decent bonus, too. But I was in such a hurry—I didn't care about the details. I just wanted to "get out of Dodge." The recruiters could tell. I was an easy recruit. I was actually supposed to go in as a Private First Class because of a buddy enlistment with my brother. But both he and my friend backed out at the last minute. I ended up being the only one who followed through.

When the time came, I flew out alone. They put you up in a hotel room first, then fly you out early the next morning to wherever your training is. Even though my brother and friend backed out, I knew deep down—whether it was an inner voice or some kind of guardian angel—I don't know. But something told me: *You made this commitment. It's time to go.*

When you arrive at reception, they shave your head and give you your vaccinations. The training I chose was all-male because it was a combat role. Non-combat and support jobs in the military have both males and females. The memory and telling my story, you can say, gets me a little excited, but yeah, at reception, you get your shots, your gear, and all your issued equipment. You're only supposed to be there for about forty-eight hours.

At that stage, you still see people as individuals. But then the day comes when the drill sergeants show up to march you to your barracks. That moment is called a *shark attack.* They call it that because it's designed to mentally break you down—to teach you that if you can stay mentally tough, you can make it through anything.

I had already built up some mental toughness through football and other experiences. Still, at nineteen years old, I thought I was tough—until the drill sergeants surrounded us. I was quivering in my boots. But that moment taught me something. Deep down, I knew I could handle it. I knew I was enough.

At the time, I thought I was proving something to others. But later in life, I realized I was actually proving something to myself—proving what kind of person I am and that, if I challenge myself, I do have the ability to push forward and accomplish anything. During my time in training, I ended up leading from the front and by example. I served as the platoon guide throughout basic training. That's where I first learned about selfless service, duty, honor, personal pride, and what it means to overcome fear.

I suppose you could say I was becoming an adult. I truly believe it would benefit many young adults to serve two years in the military. In many countries, military service is mandatory at age eighteen. In the U.S., it's voluntary, which brings an added sense of pride—you're joining a group that makes up only about three percent of the population. There's pride in that, even in the small things. But beyond pride, the military can also offer a way out—a chance to escape toxic environments and find a new path. There are so many opportunities and incredible jobs available through military service. Of course, back then—before I was actually in that world—I didn't realize all of this. But looking back, I can honestly say I accomplished a lot of amazing things.

There are many positives that come from making sacrifices for your country. The benefits are real—though you definitely have to work hard to earn them. And if you're savvy or can find the right support, there are organizations that help veterans access those resources. Still, I wish it were easier. That's one thing I'd change: I wish veteran benefits were more accessible.

But when I first joined, I wasn't thinking about benefits. I was trying to break free—to escape the short-term cycles I kept falling into, no matter where I lived. The same problems kept reappearing. And now I realize I was the one making the choices that led me back into those same environments. I was seeking what felt safe, what was familiar. I wasn't challenging myself or stepping outside my comfort zone. A lot of us end up doing the same thing.

Let me give an example to illustrate the difference between a structured military life and the routines of poverty or gang involvement. They operate on completely different principles—different forms of discipline, hierarchy, and purpose. For me, it all comes down to self-purpose. What is this path going to provide for me? Military life is built on strict discipline, schedules, and codes of conduct. Every action has a purpose—from training and daily routines to procedures that ensure you're always ready and operating efficiently. That includes your mind, body, and skills.

You're constantly training and improving—getting better at your job to ensure you're performing at your best when the time comes. In contrast, poverty, gang life, or the struggles of early adulthood are marked by instability. You never know what's going to happen next. You live day to day, navigating environments where survival depends on the choices you make.

Gangs impose their own rules, but they're often reactionary, rooted in power struggles—who's in charge, who does what, who's loyal, and so on. There aren't many structured growth opportunities —just a few short-term gains that often lead down a negative path. The outcomes are usually the same: prison, death, poor health, homelessness, addiction.

In contrast, anybody who serves in the military has a clear mission for everything they're going to do—sometimes even a year in advance. You'll know when you can go on leave, what training is coming, this or that. The only time it becomes unpredictable is if your unit gets activated for a mission, and even then, you usually get thirty to ninety days' notice. But in the end, it's about the meaning behind what you're doing—what you're supporting, the honor in it, and the long-term growth that comes with serving. And there's no camaraderie quite like what you find among service members. Even now, I can run into a veteran, and we'll shake hands, bump fists or elbows, and say, "Thank you for your service," because we understand the sacrifices. It's great telling stories to people, but only one veteran to another truly understands what we go through.

Many individuals caught in gang culture are trapped in short-term survival mode. They seek immediate gratification—money, girls, cars, status, protection—whatever it is. It takes precedence over any long-term goals and blocks your potential. But the ability to walk away and escape? That's already inside you. Gangs say there's brotherhood—but in truth, there's a lot of distrust. In the military, there's real brotherhood and sisterhood. It's a deep camaraderie among those who've worn the uniform, like nothing else. Soldiers have to trust their teams—because their lives literally depend on one another. That applies across all branches: Army, Navy, Marines, Air Force—it doesn't matter. Sure, we all mess with each other and talk some smack, but when it comes down to supporting each other on a mission, we're brothers and sisters in arms.

Gang life may talk about loyalty—"we've got your back," and all that—but it's fragile. Gangs are built on fear and power dynamics. Betrayal is common. And when survival's on the line, human nature kicks in. We protect ourselves first. So when there's no trust, no true brotherhood or unity—like what you find in the military or even in team sports—it's easy for everything to fall apart. I'm not saying the military is for everyone, but it's a far better option than ending up dead or behind bars for life.

Another difference hinges on leadership and growth versus

power and control. Leadership in the military is developed through training, mentorship, and a clear rank structure. From day one with your unit, there's always a mentor—an NCO (non-commissioned officer), usually a staff sergeant—who helps you get set up. You're not set up to fail. You're set up to excel. And if you really take advantage of what's offered and want something structured, I'd say the military is a great path. On top of that, your schooling can be paid for. You can choose jobs in the military that set you up for success in the civilian world. There are so many benefits that come from the leadership training, personal growth, and educational opportunities the military offers—both while you're serving and afterward, through scholarships and the GI Bill.

In contrast, leadership in poverty and gang life is often seized through force, fear, or manipulation. Authority shifts unpredictably, often leading to violent power struggles. That doesn't sound like a place I'd want to be CEO of. And so, I chose military life.

But again, I'm not telling my readers that joining the military will fix all your problems. The most important step I had to take before making that decision was to look within myself.

Military life provided structure, career progression, education benefits, and a sense of purpose. Many service members transition into productive civilian roles after completing their service. This is something worth considering. As I mentioned before, when you join, choose your job carefully. For me, I was in a hurry to get out of town. What was the fastest way? I had scored high enough on the ASVAB—the entry exam—that I could have become a dental hygienist, gone into military intelligence, or done a number of other jobs. But the option that would get me out of my situation the fastest was combat arms. So I chose that. But to each their own—if you're not rushing to escape a bad situation, please take time to consider a military job that will benefit you after your service ends.

In poverty and gang life, the path often leads to incarceration, violence, or an early death, as I keep emphasizing. Escaping that cycle is incredibly difficult without access to education, mentorship, or alternative opportunities. And that's a change I strongly believe needs to be made more accessible to everyone. If someone is truly trying to find a pathway out, they should be able to. I'm not pointing shame at anyone—certainly not anyone in this book—because we are all enough. But it's a real challenge when you're trying to find a way out, and the burden is fully on you to search, to fight your way through it.

So it comes down to this: What kind of "hard" do you want to choose? Do you want to choose the hardship of living in poverty and struggling every day? Or do you want to face the hardship of escaping it?

It's pretty simple. The military promotes self-control, responsibility, accountability, and so much more. At one point in my career, I was responsible for over $300 million worth of military equipment. That's a heavy load on anyone's shoulders. But I passed the Army's inspection with 100 percent success. And without everything I'd previously accomplished in the military, I don't think I would have ever believed I could do that. But I faced it, I took it on, and I was successful.

Gangs, on the other hand, encourage impulsive decisions driven by emotion, fear, and desperation—whether it's over drugs, turf, status, or something else. Honestly, in my view, it's silly that people fight over colors or neighborhoods or any of that. I mean, everyone on this planet—sure, there's evil in the world—but most people just want to be loved, appreciated, and told that they matter. Not yelled at, not screamed at. Though I guess some people may be used to that or even think they deserve it. But anyway, I digress. While both environments—military life and gang life—demand toughness, resilience, and a form of brotherhood, the military channels those traits into structured growth.

While gang life and poverty tend to perpetuate cycles of insta-bility and struggle, those who transition from the latter to the former often find purpose, discipline, and opportunities they never had before. I mean, don't just take my word for it—ask lots of veter-ans. Some veterans don't feel it was great, and that's valid. Everyone has their own perspective and experiences. For me, though, it was amazing. Even my oldest son is proudly serving in the military right now.

The key learning moment I want to share with you is that joining the military was a pivotal decision in my life—one driven by the desire for something greater than the environment I was in. For many years, I was just lost. Enlisting wasn't just about serving my country—it was about escaping a cycle of negativity. Whether that means poverty, toxic relationships, gang involvement, or simply feeling lost, the military offered something different. I found a deep sense of purpose, discipline, and self-respect that I hadn't experi-enced on the streets.

Sure, basic training was grueling. It was a total transformation. It took a bunch of individuals, stripped us of our old habits and mind-set, and molded us into a team. We learned to see the value in team-work, brotherhood, and lifting each other up. We became stronger mentally and physically.

The transition from civilian to soldier was jarring at first. But once I got used to the structure and understood that every action had a purpose, every expectation was clear—it left no room for excuses. There was no time for self-pity. Only the mission, the team, and the relentless push to be better than the day before. Whether that meant being woken up at two or three in the morning, or going without sleep entirely, the job still had to get done.

The contrast between military structure and the chaos of toxic environments couldn't be more extreme. On the streets, survival depended on deception, aggression, or submitting to forces beyond my control. In the military, survival depended on discipline, team-work, and resilience.

The military didn't just provide order—it gave me a code to live by. It was a code that instilled responsibility, honor, and a sense of belonging to something greater than myself. It gave me purpose. For those coming from broken homes, gang-heavy neighborhoods, or cycles of poverty, basic training was more than just initiation—it was a baptism by fire. It forged a new path, one many of us had never known. No more feeling lost or directionless.

You never know what's possible unless you truly try, and believe in yourself. No matter how steep the hill you're trying to climb, each challenge creates growth and knowledge that only *you* can truly appreciate. Only *you* know what it took to get where you want to be. But truly, it's your happiness and growth that matter.

This is your journey. Your story. Your life. Don't let anyone else write your story but you. Choose the hard things that promote growth, that give you a sense of self. You—and you alone—are the key to unlocking your potential. How hard you're willing to push yourself each day will determine the outcome.

The military offered me a way out—not just physically, but mentally—replacing chaos with clarity, hopelessness with ambition, and isolation with brotherhood. I mean, truly, if you're surrounded by people you think are lifting you up, pay attention. Are they there when you're laughing *and* crying, or only around when life is great? Start surrounding yourself with people who are on the path you want to be on. Find mentors, keep learning, and never feel like you're too big to open your mind and your heart.

Sometimes we have to empty our cup. That decision for me wasn't just about a career. It was about breaking free, rewriting my story, emptying my cup, clearing the page, and opening myself up to new ideas, to change—spiritual change, personal growth, everything. And I'll tell you, to this day, it was the best decision I ever made. If you're stuck in a toxic environment, trapped in poverty, or feeling the pull of destructive influences—here's some real advice, straight from someone who's been there, done that, and got the T-shirt.

When I learned how to be a good leader, it came through leading by example. You earn more support and loyalty from your team when you're willing to get your hands dirty and work alongside them. Show them you're not above the work they do—that you're in the trenches with them, leading the way. That doesn't mean doing everything yourself. It means empowering each team member, recognizing their strengths, and building their confidence. That's how you do things the right way—by being someone others can look up to.

Always be the one pushing yourself the hardest, so when you ask more of others, you're never asking more than you're willing to give yourself. Lead from the front. Let your actions speak louder than words. Grind hard in silence. Not everyone in your life has your best interests at heart. Evil lurks everywhere. You need to follow your heart and what makes you feel truly happy and blessed.

I want to share an experience that taught me a lot about what leadership *shouldn't* look like. It wasn't the hardest experience I've had, but it stuck with me. I was a Private First Class, fresh to my unit. There was this sergeant I was supposed to look up to. But every time we went out on missions in the field, he'd chew tobacco and spit on the floors of our Humvees. Then, when we got back, we had to do maintenance—including cleaning the floors. He'd hand us a bucket and sponge and tell us to clean up *his* side of the vehicle.

That was the first time I realized—this is *not* the kind of leader I want to be. To me, that behavior was garbage. If someone tells you to mop up their spit, they have no respect for you. And if you want to be a real leader, you have to respect your team. It doesn't matter if you're the director of an operation or a team lead—the lowest-ranking person should feel like they can come to you, speak to you, and be treated with the same respect as anyone else.

And that's been my philosophy ever since that day. I swore I'd be a sergeant who led from the front—by example. I used to love it when my soldiers would try to get me to stop working on vehicles and say, "We've got it, Sergeant Slade," and I'd always say, "Why? Because stripes mean I can't work on equipment anymore?" That's my perspective on true leadership. True leaders don't stand at the top of the hill and shout orders for others to drag a rock up. They grab the rope and help their team pull that rock to the top.

The following are the major insights I derived from these experiences:

1. **Decide that you want more.** No one is coming to save you. I know that sounds harsh, but it's the truth. The first step is deciding that you want a different life. That means being honest about where you are—and recognizing that staying in the same place will only give you more of the same results.

2. **Consider the military as a path to structure and opportunity.** The military isn't just about combat. It's about discipline, education, and growth. If you're looking for a way out of a bad situation, it can offer a structured path to success—whatever your goals may be, whether it's special operations, military intelligence, or another field. From college tuition and certifications to a steady paycheck, financial stability, even housing—the benefits are real. You'll find a brotherhood and sisterhood that can replace toxic influences.

Most people around you are there to support your growth. Sure, not everyone in the military is good—but if you pay attention and watch the ones who are rising, those are the people you want to build with. The same goes for the civilian world: find the people who are growing. Become friends. Get advice. Take advice

3. **If you do decide to join the military, prepare for basic training like your life depends on it—because, in many ways, it does.** The military will help break bad habits, but you don't have to wait for day one to start that transformation. Start now. Get in shape. Start running. Do push-ups. Work on endurance. Develop mental toughness. Read about military training. Push through challenges and embrace discomfort. Learn discipline. Wake up early. Stick to a routine. Hold yourself accountable.

4. **Cut dead weight.** Toxic friends, gang ties, bad habits— they won't fit in your rucksack. Let them go. This is about *your* future. If people in your life aren't supporting your

growth, they're holding you back. Let them go and make the hard choice to move forward—because, in the end, it's about *you* and your happiness.

5. **Remember, the streets don't love you.** There's no retirement plan in the streets. No benefits. No future. I know I've been preaching a bit here, but the military gives you a mission, a purpose—a way to build something real. But only if you're willing to commit. I'm not saying the military is the only way to escape hardship. Trust me, there are other paths. But you have to remember: *you are enough* to do it.

6. **Embrace the change and push through.** If you do join the military, basic training is going to test you. It's designed to break you down and build you up. But that's exactly what you need. When things get tough, remember why you started. It's not about where you came from, it's about where you're going. We learn from the lessons of the past. We don't look backward—we keep hope for the future, but we focus on the now and what we need to accomplish in order to reach that future we're envisioning. If you feel trapped, know that there is a way out. The choice is truly yours. Step up and take it.

Chapter 6 Challenge: Unplug and Reconnect

For this chapter's challenge, I recommend that you *unplug* and *reconnect*: commit to twenty-four hours without social media. Use that time to reconnect with your family, read, or engage in a hobby. Journal your thoughts at the end of the day and reflect on how it made you feel mentally, spiritually, and emotionally. It's powerful to take time to reflect and meditate on what really matters.

_____

_____

_____

_____

QUESTIONING PURPOSE DURING MY MILITARY SERVICE

A s I mentioned earlier, one of my first leaders was not a great example of how to lead soldiers. Unfortunately, this same guy ended up being my sergeant in charge during my first deployment.

Some of you may remember this, some of you may not have been born yet—but I'm talking about the conflict in Bosnia between the Bosnians and the Serbians, when Serbians were killing Bosnian Muslims. American forces were deployed essentially as a show of force—we set up bases and maintained a presence. I was deployed as part of Task Force Eagle in 1999 at Camp McGovern.

Bosnia is a beautiful country. The culture, the landscape—everywhere I've traveled in the military, I've seen beauty. But just like in America, there's also evil around us everywhere. Still, I can tell you this: there's no place like America. Nothing compares to stepping back onto American soil. If you ever get the chance to travel abroad, I guarantee you'll feel the same. There are beautiful places in the world, yes—but there's nothing quite like being back home. There are so many things we take for granted here.

For example, I saw firsthand that many women there didn't have access to basic sanitary supplies. They had to roll up socks to use in place of sanitary napkins. And trust me—when you're on gate duty and conducting searches, it's not fun to come across a used one. I'm not trying to gross anyone out, just trying to put things in perspective—to show how good we really have it in America and how easily we can overlook those daily blessings. There were times during my service when I asked myself: *What's the purpose? Why are we even here? Why are we doing a show of force if we can't stop what's happening?* When sniper shots are still being taken at us, and all we do is drive around in an up-armored Humvee all day long? And then, on top of that, once a week, you've got to scrub out your sergeant's spit from the driver's seat.

By the end of that deployment, I can tell you honestly—most of our team wouldn't have taken a bullet for that NCO (non-commissioned officer). And that alone caused a lot of internal conflict for me in my role. Because I just wanted to be positive. I tried to redirect the negativity, to remind our team: *Yes, this sucks. Yes, it's wrong that he does this. Yes, that order might be questionable.* But as a junior enlisted soldier, you often feel like your word will never matter more than a sergeant's—because *they're supposed to lead.* They're the backbone of the Army. They're the leaders. So, is it really just a bunch of junior enlisted soldiers complaining that this sergeant is being too hard? Or does it go back to that old mentality of "Men are supposed to be tough—quit being a crybaby and just get stuff done?"

But the truth is, standing up for yourself isn't complaining. It's standing up for your rights—for what you believe in deep down.

Looking back at those moments, I realize I should've stood up for myself many times during that period with that NCO. That time created a deep moral and ethical struggle for me. I had to dig deeper—to look at the beauty of the country I was in, to remember what our intent was, even though it was hard to see the value when we couldn't intervene and help people in obvious need. That's what I had thought the military was about—helping. That's what we're trained to do. That's supposed to be our mission.

Of course, I'm not saying that the United States should be the big brother to every country or that we should jump in and rescue everyone. We've got a lot to take care of right here at home. I'm not trying to take a political stance here. What I'm saying is—don't let yourself get sucked into the darkness. There were moments when I could've easily gone down a destructive path. During your military service—or in any career path, really—you'll face moments of doubt. You'll ask yourself: *Why am I here?* All the long days, the sacrifice, the demands—it adds up. And doubt creeps in.

It's not a lie. We all feel it at some point. You start questioning everything: *Why am I doing all this extra work? Why am I going through these struggles? Why are things the way they are?* And that's when I had to start reflecting inward—finding positives, finding purpose. Instead of letting my mind wander or becoming idle, I turned to training, studying, and staying productive on base.

That's what helped me get through that deployment—and many other challenges in life. Military life is relentless. Sometimes we got only four hours of sleep, followed by eighteen-hour missions. You're driving around in a constant state of exhaustion. Between the repetition and the ever-present demand to stay mentally and physically sharp, you can't help but ask: *Is this really all worth it?* There were days I didn't want to get out of bed. But in those moments, I had to dig deeper and find something bigger than myself.

Why should I lie in bed? What purpose would that serve? I need to get up. I need to keep the mission going.

Missing your family, wanting to see your friends back home—and then seeing people living "normal" lives while you're enduring hardships most people can't even imagine—it can make you feel incredibly isolated. I get that. I recognize that feeling. I've been there. And I know the moral and ethical dilemmas that come with that kind of service.

Some of us question the larger mission. We question the orders we follow. We question the real impact of our service. To anyone going through that, I would say: *Don't regret your decisions.* Learn from the lessons. Learn from the hard challenges you've faced. Look at your accomplishments. Look at what you've overcome. And remember: nothing that has happened in your life should ever prevent you from having a successful future.

I mean, sure—I may still be able to walk and have both my arms and everything else. But my brain went through some serious mental turmoil. That time marked the beginning of it. One of the things I had to do to navigate my self-doubt was remember *why* I started. When things got hard, I had to go back to that question: *Why?* Was I building a better life? Did I feel a sense of purpose? Was I serving something greater than myself? And sure, our reasons might change and evolve —but the most important thing is that we ground ourselves.

We're often reaching higher, reaching for the heavens—but think of yourself like a tree. Trees grow tall, but only after they ground themselves with deep roots. That's what we need to do, too: remember that you're enough, stay grounded, and *then* reach. Once you build that solid foundation, you can grow stronger branches—reaching wider and further.

I would also encourage you to focus on your team. The people you're serving with matter. One of the strongest forces in military life is that sense of brotherhood and sisterhood—the trust, the bond, the camaraderie I've talked about so much. You can find that, too. Maybe you already have good friends, mentors, coaches—whoever it may be, whatever your age is as you read this. Trust me, there's someone out there for each of us who can guide us—*if* we're willing to listen, take advice, and work hard for it. And even when my purpose felt unclear, just serving next to the people around me *felt* like enough.

I could never let them down. Never. I could never let the people to my left and right down. Call it masculinity, call it compassion for human life—whatever it is, once I'd gone through the training, the camaraderie, the shared struggle—I just couldn't let anyone down. So sure, some things suck. But there's a saying in the Army: "Embrace the suck." You've got to lean into it. If you're willing, you're able. It comes down to willpower.

At the end of the day, it's about believing that *you are enough.* So shift your perspective. Remember how resilient you are, the leader you're becoming, the discipline you're building. All of these qualities will carry over into whatever path you take—whether it's a career in the military, becoming a high school teacher, a coach—whatever it is. Find something that brings you joy and purpose in what you're going after.

The military shaped my future. But that doesn't mean it has to shape yours. Find *your* path—one that brings small wins. Because your dreams will always stay dreams unless you challenge yourself.

If all you do is sit and watch movies, then yeah—don't expect anything to change. If you want growth, you've got to push.

Find meaning in small wins. Some moments will feel pointless. I know. But until you stop and recognize how much you've grown, those small moments *will* feel meaningless. You have to dig deep and realize that every challenge you overcome, every skill you build, every lesson you learn—that all adds up. It gives you tools to lead. Or, at the very least, it gives you skills to carry through life. Whether it's something simple like learning how to tie knots or something bigger—it's something. Something that provides value. Something that makes you feel useful and proud. Something that allows you to give back to your community—and not just serve yourself.

But in the end, it's about *you*—your happiness, your sense of worth, and knowing that you're enough and you're capable. And it's also about talking about it. Just like I'm doing with you in this book—you're not alone. Find a mentor, a battle buddy, or someone who has been through challenges—whether it's military-related or something else entirely. Find someone who's willing to share. You can gain so much clarity just through conversation and hearing another person's perspective. Keep your mind open.

Like I've said before, sometimes you have to dump out the cup to truly see things differently. We're not all in the same box. We don't all think the same way. But in general, we *can* understand one another—especially when we talk with people who've *been there* and *get it*. Sometimes, just hearing that someone else has gone through what you're going through can make all the difference. It can give you the strength to move forward.

Sure, there were moments when I made poor choices that caused me to move backward in rank during my military service. But I owned up to them—and that ownership allowed me to move forward again. The best advice I can give my readers is this: *look at the bigger picture.* Doubt is normal. Trust me, I still struggle with doubt, too. But that doesn't mean you're weak. It just means you're thinking critically about your life and your mission.

The key is not to let temporary emotions lead to permanent decisions. Get control of your emotions *before* you make any big choices. And never—*never*—make decisions out of anger. Anger comes from fight-or-flight mode. And when we're in that state, it's like letting go of the reins on a horse-drawn buggy after the horses just got spooked by a snake—you're no longer in control. Things can come out that you'll regret later, I promise you. Take time to cool off. Walk it off. Meditate. Count to ten. Do whatever you need to do. But in the end, make decisions with a clear, conscious mind. When you're pushing through and redefining your purpose—if that's what you need right now—just keep moving forward.

And remember: *you are enough.* Because when you look back, you'll see that this journey has shaped you in ways you could never have imagined.

I believe reflection is a powerful tool—not to judge ourselves, but to understand that we are *not* the same person we were yesterday. If you look back and judge, rather than learn, you'll always feel regret. But if you look at the *value* of the lessons you've learned—even when the lessons came from mistakes—then you'll see how far you've come.

For example, I once chose to follow a negative pattern during a deployment that caused me to spiral into a dark place—I questioned my morality, my ethics, and the meaning behind the mission. But in the end, yes—leaving family and friends behind was worth it. Had I let my emotions take over? No—I could have become bitter, angry, and consumed by negativity like everything else around me. But instead, I paid attention. I saw that life brings *lessons* and *blessings*.

Even just starting your day with gratitude—being thankful that you opened your eyes, that you're breathing, that your body is functioning—those small things matter. Then you start recognizing the world around you: *I can get up. I can walk. I can move.* And slowly but surely, you begin to awaken to more positive energy and start seeing life from a new perspective. You *can* do it. It starts with your mindset.

I can honestly say: I *know* these things. But even now, I sometimes fall back into those dark holes. I still have days when I feel like I can't even communicate properly with other people. And I want to just stay in bed. You know, those are the days I have to tell myself: *Nope. We're getting up. We need sunshine. We need more than just lying in bed and letting our minds spiral into the darkness—rehashing all the would-haves, should-haves, and could-haves from the past.* I know my lessons now.

And yes, I've apologized for many of the bad choices I made to the people who truly deserved an apology (I'm not saying *everyone* gets one). You also have to learn to forgive yourself. That's number one. I've had to keep working on it, and I challenge you to do the same.

Just remember: ultimately, *you* are the creator of your environment. Whether it's a toxic space, or a difficult season where your goals don't seem to be going as planned—trust me, that's just resistance trying to get you to quit. Why? Because what you're pushing yourself to do is *great.* But here's the hard truth: only about four percent of people actually achieve 100 percent of their dreams and goals. That's because most people let the shadows—doubt, fear, and darkness—stop them from moving forward. But not you. Not me. I know I'm responsible for *me*.

I'm responsible for my feelings, my results, and the outcomes of my choices. Let your *actions* be your noise. Don't brag, don't shout —let your work speak for itself. Move quietly toward your goals. Then, when you emerge—whether you call it coming out of a cocoon, becoming a butterfly, or stepping into your new self—be proud of that transformation. Many of us have been through it. For me, this was one of the most mentally challenging times—along with many of my other deployments. But in the end, I realized: *We are enough. You* are enough. *We* are all unique.

Every challenge placed in front of us has a purpose. I truly believe that we each have a path on this planet. The hard path seems tough in the beginning—but it often leads to an easier, happier, fuller life in the end. The "easy" path up front? That's the one that often leads to homelessness, jail, financial or mental struggles, or just falling short of the life you really want. Are you going to let all that negativity consume you and block you from seeing the blessings that are already within reach? Don't look at a closed door as the end. See it as another opportunity waiting to be opened.

Chapter 7 Challenge: The "Fuel Your Body" Challenge

For one week, I challenge you to commit to fueling your body properly: Eat wholesome, nutrient-dense foods. Hydrate well. Eliminate processed junk food. Then, reflect on how your body responds— because your *stomach* is your second brain. A lot of people don't realize that 95 percent of your happy hormones are produced in your gut. That's why I'm offering you this challenge: if you're struggling mentally, physically, or emotionally—especially with digestion or energy—I guarantee that if you take this challenge seriously, you will feel amazing after just one week.

FAMILY, LOVE, AND RELATIONSHIP CHALLENGES

U nfortunately, too many military service members have to deal with infidelity—whether it's from a spouse or a girl-friend. Sometimes it's the soldier's actions, and sometimes it's their partner's. I don't know what goes on in other people's lives, but in mine, I was simply trying to be a good, faithful husband and father while serving.

Unfortunately, before I returned from vacation during my military service, I had a short-term relationship with a woman back home, and later discovered that I had a son who was already two years old. The way I found out was by being served with papers through our state's child support service, called the Office of Recovery Services.

That's how I first learned about him. I had no idea about his existence until he was two. At that time, I was away on my first duty station, serving in the military. As I mentioned, the relation-ship had been short—just a fling. I was confused as to why the woman had never let me know earlier. Yes, I would've still questioned it, but the outcome would have been the same: I would have wanted to know I was a father at twenty-two. It wasn't part of my plan to become a parent so young—but kids don't always arrive according to plan. Still, I can tell you this: becoming a father has been one of the greatest blessings of my life.

It wasn't something I had seriously thought about at that time. I was like most people: we play the game, we make choices. That was one of mine—an adult decision. If I had created a son, then I was willing to be his father and support him in any way I could. But there were struggles too. Two years down the road, I was served child support papers while living in Texas and still actively serving in the military.

Naturally, I had questions, not because I didn't want to be a dad (I *was* excited to be a dad), but because I wanted to be sure. I truly wanted to step into the role of fatherhood. I don't know many men who openly talk about wanting to be a father, but for me, even as a young boy, it was a dream. I wanted to grow up, get married, have a family, and be a dad. I grew up in a big family, surrounded by brothers, and a sister, and I loved that environment. So yes, I wanted to support my child—but I needed to be certain he was mine. I requested DNA testing. Long story short: the DNA proved the little boy was my son.

At the time, I was married to a woman I had dated on and off throughout high school. We were already going through our own struggles. Looking back now, I can admit: I probably should have listened to my parents' advice and never married her, let alone moved her to Texas with me. They could see what I couldn't—that we probably weren't good for each other. We just weren't right together. We were both still young, and I can see that clearly now.

That said, I'm civil with her today. I can speak to her and her husband respectfully and calmly. And yes, my adult children and grandchildren are currently living in her basement because times are tough economically. But despite everything, I didn't listen to my parents then. I brought my high school girlfriend with me to Texas. It was during that time, as I mentioned earlier in this chapter, that I discovered my firstborn son after being served those child support papers.

I was also undergoing intense training then because the unit I was in was designated as the president's "first call." Basically, if things went bad, our unit was the first to deploy, with a moment's notice from the commander-in-chief. We were the first ones out of the gate. We spent about eight months of the year training in the field, with only about four months total back at home. Still, you had a guaranteed block leave—two weeks during Christmas and two weeks in mid-summer. Block leave had to be scheduled and approved in advance. But back then, I was just a poor private— junior enlisted—trying to make ends meet. Even with military stipends and allowances, I was barely scraping by. And now I had to pay child support on top of rent and everything else.

I couldn't afford plane tickets back then. It would've actually been cheaper to drive the twenty-one hours home. Long story short, during one of my training rotations, I came home and discovered that my wife at the time had been unfaithful. This wasn't just a single act of infidelity. She had been involved with multiple men during my time away in the field. I'm not saying this to speak poorly about her. Like I've said before, we're in a good enough place now that we can say hello and be civil. I can pick up my grandson from her house. There's no animosity between us today. But back then, when I found out, I bought her a bus ticket and sent her back to Utah. I also asked the guy who had been around to never come back again.

To this day, I choose to be forgiving. I believe people's choices are just that—their own. When something negative happens in your life, it's not always your fault alone. Everyone involved has a choice. Their actions speak louder than words.

I reflected a lot on my military career during that time. Her cheating had *nothing* to do with me—my character or my self-worth. Those two people made their own decisions. I didn't force anything. I didn't create that betrayal. Despite everything, I still tried to work things out. I've always believed that if you commit to something, you need to do the work to honor that commitment. I had strong examples in my life. My parents, at the time of writing this book, have been married for forty-nine years. I saw firsthand what it meant to work through differences, challenges, and hardship. So, I tried. I really did. But deep down—it was hard.

And then, I found out she was pregnant. We went all the way to childbirth thinking this was my child. I was flown home from the Army because she had returned to Utah, and I wanted to be there. I was hopeful—truly hoping this was my biological son. When he was born, even my mother was there. People tried to reassure me, saying the baby had jaundice and that's why he looked the way he did—that he was mine. But I could see it. Deep down, I knew. It was clear the child wasn't biologically mine. He had her DNA, yes. But not mine. And when I realized that, I struggled. I stepped out into the hallway, took a deep breath, and had to say to myself: *Okay. Wow.*

You know, not only had I just found out I had a two-year-old son —but now I had a newborn son who wasn't biologically mine. I was a young twenty-four-year-old man, and I had to ask myself: *Do I walk away from this? Do I leave the relationship? Do I walk away from this innocent child? Or do I try to see if I can make things work?* And you know, my mother—who I love dearly—has always been a guiding voice in my life. If you have a mother who offers that kind of support and wisdom, be truly grateful. Sure, sometimes our mothers can sound like they're nagging or pecking at us, but at the heart of it, most moms just want to love their children and see them succeed.

Growing up, I was smart enough, most of the time, to listen to my mother. She mentored me a lot. During that moment at the hospital, she pulled me aside into the hallway and gently told me, "I know this child is not your biological son—you can see it yourself." But then she said something that changed my life. She said, "I want you to think about what kind of life this child will have if you don't stay and choose to become his father." So ultimately, I made the decision that I would be this newborn baby boy's father. In Utah, under marriage law, if a child is born while a couple is still legally married and the biological father does not come forward, the husband can legally sign the birth certificate. At that time, she didn't know who the biological father was.

Today, I refer to him as the sperm donor, the biological donor—whatever you want to call him. But back then, he wasn't in the picture. So I signed the birth certificate and named the child after me. I didn't do it out of spite or to prove a point. I did it because I was committing to love and protect this child as my own. He was my son, regardless of biology. And despite everything, I still tried to make the relationship work—even though we were living apart. Eventually, I had my third and final child, my beautiful daughter, with the same woman—the mother of my second son. Each one of my children has been a blessing. I'm grateful for them all. But the situation brought new challenges and new beginnings. Ultimately, I walked away from that relationship.

My military assignments eventually brought me back home to Utah, where I met someone I truly thought was "the one." She seemed amazing, and in the beginning, it felt good. During that time, though, I faced a lot of poor advice and constant criticism—from friends, colleagues, even strangers. People would say things like, "I don't understand why you'd raise someone else's child," or "That's not your responsibility," and on and on. But I didn't care. He was my child. And I would give my life to see any of my children grow and flourish in this world.

Before my deployment to Iraq in 2003, I married the woman I had been dating on and off, who was now becoming a stepmother to my children. I truly believed I had found someone loyal and committed. (You'll have to keep reading the later chapters to hear how that story unfolds.) But what I want to touch on now is this: the emotional toll that infidelity and betrayal can take. It hits all of us differently. Especially those of us who are built on strong values, who give loyalty and expect loyalty in return, who commit fully—and make sacrifices—because we believe that's what love and honor require. Relationships aren't 50/50. They're about two people choosing to be a team—choosing to build something special together. And in the end, that team should be one that lifts each other up—one that you can trust with your life.

As I often use military examples, I'll say this: just like you trust the men and women in your unit with your life—any time you deploy, train, or face danger—a marriage is supposed to be *even stronger* than that. But when that trust is shattered at home—whether in a marriage, relationship, or any personal bond—it opens wounds none of us are ever truly prepared for. It creates anger.

Animosity. Frustration. Deep self-doubt. So many painful emotions come from betrayal. Discovering a spouse's infidelity, for example, isn't just about the act itself. It's about the *breaking* of a sacred trust —a safety, a belief that all the sacrifices you made were for something real, something solid. For that team.

I was away, serving, providing, dedicating myself to duty. Meanwhile, the home that was supposed to be my safe space was crumbling behind my back without my knowledge. That kind of betrayal cuts deeply—not only because of the pain it causes, but because of the ripple effects it creates. Like I said: the doubt, the anger, the endless questions: *Was this relationship ever real? Was I just a placeholder? Was I being used?* Some people will throw it back at you (i.e., *What did you even have that I could use?*), but that's what betrayal creates: self-doubt. A mental battle. You're trying to stay focused on your mission, your career, your responsibilities—while your personal world is falling apart. I wouldn't wish that kind of pain on anyone.

And if you've gone through it—I feel you. I truly do. But please remember: *you are enough.* Whatever you're struggling with— whether it's something like this or something even heavier—know that your pain is valid. I'm not here to say someone else's pain is worse or lighter. I'm not you. I can't determine your scale. But I can remind you: *you matter.* Yes, it takes two people in any relationship. But everyone is responsible for their own actions—their choices, their decisions. No one else is to blame for how you choose to *respond* to another's behavior. That's yours. And there's power in owning that.

When you learn to understand where your feelings come from, and when you can remain grounded in the middle of emotional chaos—that's where strength is born. Be the duck. On the surface, the duck looks calm, gliding across the water. But underneath, its feet are paddling like crazy. We don't see that. We just see serenity. But that duck is always alert—aware of dangers from above or below —but it keeps moving. Another lesson from the duck: when water hits, it rolls right off its back. Life will throw things at you. Let it roll off. If your shoulders weren't meant to carry a burden, don't force yourself to hold it. Own your *own* faults—but don't carry what isn't yours. And above all—love yourself. Believe that you are enough.

It's not what you're going through. It's how you respond to what you're going through. That's what reveals your true character. You are not your past. You are not your wounds. You are how you rise from them. Good, bad, painful—those are just *lessons learned*. It's not about the event. It's about what you *did* with it. How you reacted. How you moved forward. And I say all this not to brag—but to share what I've lived. It's to remind you that *you're enough*. I share my challenges because I want people to know there are millions of us out there—just like you—struggling every day. But we all have it within us, if we would just believe in ourselves and push past the fear factory. Remember: we're enough.

Embracing a child and building a blended family—through the wreckage of that situation—brought something unexpected: love in a different form. I had a choice. I could've become bitter and walked away from everything, or I could stand up and be a man for an innocent child caught in the middle.

I chose the latter, as I've said before. That child became mine— not by blood, but by something even stronger: *commitment*. And I'm so grateful I made that decision. I would never change that choice.

Being a father—though I've never been perfect and never will claim to be—has taught me a lot. We grow together. We learn through our experiences. But I definitely wanted to parent differently than how I was raised. I wanted to raise my children with *empowerment*, to remind them that *they are enough*, that they should chase the stars but also stay grounded. And you, too, have that ability.

Being a father has been one of the most precious blessings of my life. And from there, life had more plans for me. Down the road, more children came—each bringing a deeper sense of purpose. I realized that family isn't just about DNA. It's about showing up. It's about leading. It's about loving—no matter what.

Building a blended family wasn't easy. The struggles of parenting, the baggage from past hurts, and the complexities of different family dynamics tested my patience, my resilience, and my ability to keep my heart open when I wanted to shut it all down. Even though all my children are grateful, and I'm honored to be their father, I know there were times I wasn't fully present for them.

Looking back, I should have taken a breath, stepped away from the chaos, and made more time. Sure, I played with them. I was there in moments. But I also know that some of my children still carry hurt from my absence—especially because of my military service. I wasn't there for some of the struggles they went through, and that pains me. Looking back, I'm proud of my service—but I also understand they didn't fully grasp the sacrifices I was making. And it tore me up inside, mentally and emotionally, every time I had to leave those little ones behind.

Still, I've always tried to remind them that *they are enough*. I've done my best to put distractions aside and focus on our time together. Children are just little people who haven't learned everything yet. So—be patient. Take a breath. Walk away if you have to.

But *show up* for your kids, for children, for the people who need you.

After the heartbreak of that failed relationship, I did what a lot of people do: I threw myself into work. The military became my escape, my structure, my sense of control. I knew my schedule. I knew what to expect. So when my personal life felt chaotic and out of control, I doubled down on work. Deployments? I volunteered. Extra responsibilities? I took them. Long hours? I embraced them. It was easier for me to face the battlefield—literally—than to face my own emotions. It was easier to focus on the mission than to admit that I was breaking inside. And for a long time, that worked.

But here's the truth about running: Eventually, you get tired. And when you get tired, you crash. I hope that you find your *turning point* before that final crash. Because the real battles I had to face—those weren't overseas or in training. It was about facing my own pain—my mistakes, my feelings—and learning how to understand them. I had to stop running. I couldn't keep drowning myself in work, alcohol, or all the other things I used to numb myself. I had to stop avoiding and start healing. I had to rebuild—not just as a soldier, but as a man, a father, and someone who refused to let past wounds define the future. I had to move forward. And what gave me my *why* was my children.

From the moment they were born, my children have always been my driving force—to keep going, to lead from the front. Granted, I wasn't perfect. And I fully recognize that. I'm not too proud, too tough, or too old to say it—I've apologized to every single one of my children. For not being there enough when I was away. For not being present when they were scared. For the times I was home physically but not there mentally because of my own internal pain. Young children don't always understand the weight we carry—the emotional bricks stacked on their parents' shoulders.

Some of the time, they knew their dad had gone through bad relationships. They were even relieved when I left one of them. And I eventually got full custody of my two youngest children—ages four and five. Becoming a full-time father to them was an incredible blessing. But that other failed relationship? That woman was cruel to my children. And I didn't see it clearly at the time. That experience taught me one of the most valuable lessons of all: *you can't blame yourself for everything.* Yes, I was part of the problem. I was burying myself in work, thinking I was escaping a failed relationship, but I wasn't seeing how my pain—and my absence—was affecting my children. Looking back, I would do anything to fix that.

But I wouldn't change my children. I wouldn't undo the journey. Because every single thing I've gone through—every lesson, every heartbreak, every moment—has been a blessing in its own way. Whether through what it taught me, or through the gift of my children being brought into this world. So, if you're reading this, and you're struggling with betrayal… If you're trying to build a blended family… If you've been burying your pain in work, distractions, or addictions… This part of my story is for *you*. I want to help you stop running from the pain. Because if we run too long, some of us eventually just give up—on ourselves, and on life. And that is something I understand all too well. Yes, it hurts. Yes, life hits hard. And yes, there are days when it feels like you want to give up. But please— don't. Don't take your life. There is a way out. There is a positive way out of the darkness.

If you've been betrayed—whether through infidelity, abandonment, or emotional wounds—it cuts deep. Infidelity, especially, isn't just a betrayal of trust. It strikes at your identity, your confidence, and everything you thought was solid. But here's the truth: Their actions do not define your worth. Feel the pain. Don't numb it. Don't bury it in distractions, alcohol, or anger. Own your emotions. Let yourself *feel* them. Let yourself *process* them. That's how you let go—by letting it pass through you, not harden inside you.

Don't let betrayal make you bitter or closed off. Don't tell yourself you've been cheated out of a good life or that you got the short end of the stick. And don't let one person's actions define how you see everyone else. What *one* person did doesn't mean *everyone* will do the same. And as you keep trying to focus and move toward more positive things, life will begin to present more positive gifts in return. But being closed off only punishes *you*, not anyone else. It's like drinking poison and hoping the person you're mad at gets sick from it.

Move forward with purpose. Forgiveness doesn't mean forgetting—it means refusing to let someone else's choices dictate your future.

Don't allow yourself to fall into the trap of saying, "This is who I am," or "I'm not worthy," or "They did this *because* of me." No. They made those choices because of who they are. You are not defined by their actions. Rise above the flames. Become something *amazing*, something forged in fire.

Because love isn't just a feeling—it's a *choice*. And family isn't just about blood. Blended families come with challenges, yes. But love is about *commitment*, not DNA.

Just remember: be consistent. Kids don't need perfection. They need your presence. We're here to love them, to guide them—not to hover over them, but to *be there*. Let them take on challenges. Let them try and stumble. But be there to support them when they need it. Drop the "not-my-kid" mindset. If you step into that role, *step in fully.*

As my grandmother used to say: "Why show up to a job if you're not going to give 100 percent?" Let go of resentment. If you're parenting a child from a tough situation, don't let their past dictate your relationship. Show up. Show love.

Now, let's talk about avoidance. It's easy to dive into work, the gym, deployments—anything that keeps your mind off the pain. I call this *robot mode* You're just going through the motions, focusing only on tasks that don't require emotional energy. Sure, working out takes physical effort, but it can be a distraction too—just like work. Most men can only focus on one thing at a time. That's not a criticism—it's a biological fact.

Scientifically, men have less neural connectivity between brain hemispheres, which is why women are such great multitaskers. Men, on the other hand, tend to open one box at a time—and when a box is painful, we shove it to the back of the shelf. But eventually, I promise you—if you keep avoiding it—you'll *crash*. And if that crash leads you to a place where you're questioning your worth or your life, I pray you'll remember this: **Don't give up.**

I've had my face in the mud. I've been there. I know how hard it gets. I've questioned my own reasons for staying alive. But trust me: You are enough. You have value. Just take a deep breath. Breathe in the air. And keep going. You have to face what's hurting you. Running only delays the healing. Once you get it off your chest— once you confront the pain and truly process it—you'll feel lighter.

And listen: You don't have to forgive the person who hurt you. But you do have to let go of what's weighing you down. Learn the lesson. Release the burden. Find balance.

Yes, work and purpose matter. But they're not a substitute for real healing. Make time for joy. Go to therapy. Take walks in nature. Sit in silence. Reflect. Whatever helps you—*do it*. Make the time. And please, don't use work to avoid new relationships. You might tell yourself you're too busy, but that's just fear talking. And whether or not you're seeking a new romantic relationship, I urge you to focus on *finding yourself first*.

Heal yourself first. Love yourself first, and you will find an amazing, like-minded partner and everything else will follow. If you are searching while you're in the dark, you're going to find somebody in the dark, and they may not necessarily climb out of the darkness with you. It may just be another horrible downward spiral. I'm not saying that people who feel down on their luck can't rise out of the ashes together, but build something that lasts. After everything in life, we ultimately have two choices: we can stay bitter and closed off, or we can build a future stronger than the past. I chose to build. I strongly urge you to choose to build.

Always move forward—always forward—and always believe that you're enough to do that. Lead your family or your team, or whatever it may be, with strength and love. Love is an action word. Love is all the actions of caring. Love is not an emotion. Love is the very definition of everything you do to show that you care.

Be the foundation that people can count on. Take control of your own healing through therapy, faith, mentorship, or whatever helps you grow. Do it, because that's the only way you'll ever see things in a different light. Take control of yourself.

Redefine success. It's not about proving people wrong; it's about building a life you're proud of. If you're going at life thinking, *I'm going to show all these people,* sure, it's okay to have that drive, but choose a path that you'll be proud of. A path where, at the end of the day, you can look yourself in the mirror and say, *You know what?*

I'm proud of myself. I worked hard. I am a good person. I made the best choices I could. I worked as hard as I could within my abilities. Whatever brings you a sense of value—remember, just by breathing air, we have value. Everything else you do and provide is a skill you bring to your community. It gives you a sense of purpose, but it doesn't define your self-worth.

Never let someone else's actions control your future. Betrayal, broken relationships, tough family dynamics, growing up in poverty, your skin color—none of that defines you. How you respond to everything that happens to you in life along your path *is* you. It's you. Own your story. Embrace those struggles.

Don't be ashamed of your struggles. Embrace them. Look at what those challenges have done to make you a stronger, more resilient person—to help you know what you don't want in life, and what you *do* want. What aligns with you, and what doesn't. As you start reflecting and realizing those things, you'll see that you're not a victim. You're a warrior. And warriors never stay down. They rise above the fire and the ashes to become someone molded by the lessons learned—whether from relationships, careers, life, self-worth, health—you name it.

But truly, if you dig deep inside and believe that you are enough, and that you can be proud of yourself every day, there is nothing the universe can throw at you that you won't be able to fight through and overcome. Never give up on yourself, because at the end of the day, you're the only one who *can't* give up on you. Others may walk away when the path seems too hard, but if you're willing to keep going—because you know there's a beautiful sunrise beyond that horizon, and more beautiful sunrises after that—you won't give up.

Just keep seeing those dreams. Sometimes you have to live

through that part. But whatever helps you maintain positivity and focus—rather than getting caught up in the negative side of others' actions—do it. Go with it, run with it, move forward, and always believe that you're enough.

Chapter 8 Challenge: The Fearless Challenge

As I keep telling you, you have to do something that scares you. Public speaking, starting a new project, or facing a fear—one of those things you've been putting off forever. You think, *I really want to do this, but it's going to be hard to learn.* I don't care. Choose something you know you can accomplish—a short-term goal, whatever it may be—but something you've delayed out of fear because it seemed too hard.

It's a challenge, sure. I call that fear *the little kid inside me*—the fear factory. I don't let that little kid tell me what to do anymore. I tell that little child, *I'm a grown-up. I'm an adult. Thank you for your concern, but we're going ahead and doing this.* I mean, why be scared of jumping out of the airplane before you're actually jumping out of the airplane? It's the same philosophy. Embrace the discomfort—and then celebrate.

Give yourself a celebration for taking action for yourself, for learning something new, whatever it may be. But I challenge you: do something that scares you.

THE EXPLOSION AND LIFE-ALTERING
TURNING POINT

Countless men and women have been deployed all over the world to stand up for the freedoms of others. They defend those freedoms regardless of others' opinions or political views.

Speaking for myself, I tell everyone who asks: "I did not go to war out of hate for the opposing force, but out of love for the ones I was leaving behind, in the hope that my efforts would help create a safer future for everyone who truly desires safety, security, and the freedom to live, work, and worship as they wish." Some of my best memories while deployed came from engaging with local youth, working on humanitarian projects, and handing out school supplies and other items.

But, as you know, it wasn't always fun and games or playing soccer with kids. We had missions to carry out, and sometimes things went wrong. One event that really hit me—both physically and to my ego—occurred in March of 2005, while I was in Iraq, serving from OIF-1 to OIF-4.

I was there for a total of 545 days. That night, we had just completed a successful mission targeting high-ranking individuals known to be terrorists. Everything had gone according to plan. As we were preparing to return to our fire base, I chose to ride in the back of a Humvee, manning the machine gun—that's where I felt most comfortable. I was also considered the "old guy" at twenty-seven years old. The two junior enlisted soldiers with me were only nineteen and twenty, and I felt it was safer for them to be seated inside the up-armored portion of the vehicle.

The Humvee rumbled forward, kicking up dust on an Iraqi road like so many others we had traveled. It was unforgiving, unpredictable, and riddled with unseen dangers. I had been on countless patrols before, but war has a way of making every mission feel both routine and like it could be your last—especially when the enemy doesn't wear a uniform or follow traditional combat tactics.

The terrorists we confronted aimed to spread fear through violence and explosives, to cause chaos and destruction on a large scale, to instill fear in the masses. On the way back to the fire base— we always varied our routes—I manned the machine gun once again, letting the younger guys ride in the more protected space. This was during the time Donald Rumsfeld was requesting more armored vehicles for our troops. We simply didn't have enough. We weren't truly prepared for what these terrorists were bringing to the fight, and we lacked the equipment to match the threat. Still, we made do with what we had, and I felt confident behind the machine gun. It was one of my favorite weapons to operate.

And then, in an instant, everything changed. The deafening roar of an IED explosion shattered the moment. The vehicle was consumed by a violent shockwave. Time slowed, yet everything happened at once. Searing heat. A force like a hammer slammed into my body. Debris splintered everywhere. The air filled with smoke, dust, and the acrid stench of burning rubber and blood.

You know that coppery taste you get from a bloody nose? That's what I tasted. I felt myself being thrown, my body no longer under my control. Pain erupted everywhere—sharp, brutal, unforgiving. My ears rang with a high-pitched whine, drowning out the shouts and chaos around me. My vision blurred, but I could make out figures moving—brothers-in-arms responding. Training kicked in as they ran to me, where I was slumped against the side of the Humvee.

Amazingly, it was still operational after being hit with an IED. My body was bruised and beaten, but my mind was reeling even more. Lying there, bleeding into the dirt of a foreign land, one thought after another pulsed through my head. *Is this it? Is this how it ends? What about my children? How's the rest of the team?* But it didn't end there. The medics worked fast, stabilizing me as best they could. The pain was overwhelming, but adrenaline kept me conscious, aware of every second of my new reality.

The evacuation was swift, but each moment felt like an eternity. The weight of what had just happened began to settle in, but the full magnitude of my injuries wouldn't hit me until later. I had faced danger before. I had trained for this. But training couldn't prepare me for what came next—a long road to recovery. A battle not fought with weapons, but with willpower, resilience, and an unshakable refusal to be defined by the damage.

I was patched up, had three false teeth put in, and returned to duty after being placed on light duty—mainly radio work at the fire base—for thirty days. What saved me, besides what I believe were angels—because I do believe I have guardian angels—was that the terrorists buried the IED too deep. The ground absorbed most of the blast wave, sparing me from being torn apart. What actually hit me were fragments of rock and debris, which earned me some stitches and other minor injuries. I also ended up herniating a few discs in my back—though that wouldn't be discovered until I got home.

Not long after I was cleared to go back out on patrols, Iraq was holding its first elections. That was an incredible moment—to witness a ninety percent voter turnout despite the very real threat of terrorist groups killing people on their way to the polls. It was deeply inspirational. But then I received word from a victim advocate group back home: my children were being abused while living with their mother. I was told I needed to come home and get them out of that situation—because there was no one else who could.

Despite this, the commanding general over the theater at the time decided that our mission—protecting the elections—was more important than allowing me to return home to remove my children from harm. So I had to live with the knowledge that my children were not in a safe place, all while keeping my mind focused and locked in on my mission—just so I could finish the deployment and return to save them. And for a soldier, that's not uncommon.

A lot of us face things like this—disloyalty at home, family crises, or other hardships that we can't do anything about. And if your mission is deemed that important, you're not going to change a commanding general's decision. The worst thing you can do is beat yourself up. And that's what I chose not to do. I kept telling myself, over and over again, *I'm clear across the globe, fighting a war in another country, trying to save other people.*

Yet my children weren't protected at home. And I had to turn that off in my head every single time I went out on a mission or did anything, because if I carried that burden with me—knowing my children were 12,000 miles away—I wouldn't have been able to focus on my mission. And what good would I have been to my children if I had ended up dead? So I switched into survival mode.

I focused on my fitness. I trained every day while on the fire base—two hours of working out, no matter what. I asked my wife at the time to start taking my children more often from that home, and she did, which took some of that burden off me. That part was a relief. But later on, I discovered that she wasn't treating my children well either. She would do things that were harmful or neglectful. That's another reason I walked away from that relationship. The physical injuries were one thing. But once I finally returned home after deployment, I had to deal with the long-term consequences—dozens of epidural injections. I got one every six months in my lower spine, just to keep functioning and stay in the military.

Although they discovered I had herniated discs, I could no longer serve in combat. I wasn't deployable anymore. And for someone who had trained as hard as I did—who gave everything to shine in the military—that was devastating. At first, I thought I was doing it to prove something to others because, deep down, I didn't feel like I was enough. I thought if I could just prove myself, then maybe I *would* be enough.

But when you live that way, you overstress yourself. So, I had to learn to live with the pain—and let go of something I loved. I transitioned to a combat support role and ended up specializing in chemical, biological, nuclear, and high-explosive operations. Sure, that brought its own kind of adrenaline rush, but it was support—not combat. Eventually, that led me to a new career path. I served as a recruiter for a while, became a drill sergeant for a while—I did a bit of everything.

When I came home, I thought I had a loyal partner who was caring for my children. But I found out otherwise. Our marriage was already struggling, but I discovered she had someone else on the side. Worse, she was locking my children in their rooms when she went out on dates. She did other things to them—things I still struggle to understand. My children and I have talked about it, and it's heartbreaking. But we don't always choose our partners wisely. Ultimately, I had to face the transition from being a warfighter to becoming a wounded warrior. That tested me in ways I never expected. On top of all that, I had to endure a toxic relationship with someone who constantly tore me down—told me I wasn't enough. Like so many others, I tried to smile through it, to put on a brave face in front of my kids, to raise them the best way I could. But they were too afraid to tell me what was happening when Dad wasn't there.

Eventually, I had to make a decision. I had to put my own health and well-being first. I realized that, for my sake and my children's, I needed to walk away. And the day that realization came—when the light finally broke through—I began focusing on my mental wellness. I began focusing on becoming a better dad. I started focusing on loving myself and realizing that I *am* enough. It was the day the light finally shone on me—I asked for a divorce and walked away. And yeah, that was hard in itself.

But you know, for a long time, I felt like I had come home, and rescued my children—even though I was struggling with changing jobs in the military, trying to find a new path, and trying to feel like I still had worth, especially since I could no longer go into combat. And honestly, the more time you spend in combat, the more it begins to feel like home. Most soldiers can attest to this—that feeling becomes your normal. It's unfortunate. I imagine it's similar for people who've been incarcerated. If you don't get real therapy or guidance to help you understand how we work as human beings—

how our brains work—then you'll never truly learn how to shut certain things off, let things go, and forgive. But forgiveness doesn't mean you have to associate with those people again. You forgive to release the burden and move on. I had to learn how to shut off the worries, walk away from another failed marriage, become a single dad, and go through all of that while still transitioning in the military.

I have learned lessons and blessings from all of these experiences. I would like to share this with my readers: Have patience. Trust the way things are unfolding. If you push too hard or rush too fast, things can fall apart or go terribly wrong. As I always say, "Slow is smooth, and smooth is fast."

Have faith—whether you're spiritual, religious, or not. Have *true* faith: faith in yourself. Because we are all truly made with greatness. Our bodies are amazing. Our minds are amazing. But we must believe in ourselves. No matter what social media or the world says, believe in *you*. You're not here to look like anyone else or live like anyone else. You're here to be *you*. You are one in four trillion. So always, always, always trust in yourself. Trust in your abilities. That's what I had to do—dig deep and trust in everything. And I prayed to the heavens that my children would be okay.

I'm not afraid to say I'm a spiritual person. I believe there is life beyond this planet. I believe this life is a test. But the real test is in our own heads, honestly. And I've discovered that through the trials and tribulations I've lived through. This is just the start of a new beginning.

Chapter 9 Challenge: Mindfulness Challenge

Spend five to ten minutes each day in quiet reflection, prayer, or meditation. Observe how mindfulness impacts your stress levels and clarity.

_____

_____

_____

_____

10

RETURNING HOME AND BATTLING
WITH PTSD

A s I mentioned in Chapter 9, I was dealing with a lot of drama when I came home. On top of that, I realized I was struggling with post-traumatic stress disorder—PTSD—from everything I had been through. Mentally, I truly believed that because I had survived it all, everything must be okay. I had made it through the experience, come home, gotten custody of my children, and removed them from a horrible situation. But I was still in a horrible situation—in my own mind, in my marriage, and while changing military careers. Through all of this, my mind was struggling.

I had no idea I was becoming so hyper-vigilant. Everywhere I went and everything I did—outside of work and home duties—I was basically in robot mode. At work, I could function. At home, I thought I was functioning. But in between? I was scanning rooftops, checking every corner for threats. I couldn't stand being in crowded places. Grocery shopping gave me the worst anxiety. Still, I knew I had to keep pushing myself and providing for my children. I believed that if I didn't keep going, we'd end up homeless. That fear gave me my *why*—the reason I kept going through the mental battles.

One day, I finally woke up and admitted it: I have PTSD. I didn't *want* to have PTSD. As a soldier, someone trained to be a warrior, someone taught to complete the mission even if you're the lone survivor, I couldn't believe I had let my mind "break." But did I really let it break? No—it was the weight of all the stress, the buried trauma, the things I kept pushing down and never talked about. And I'll be honest—I'm not someone who recommends group therapy. For me, group therapy meant listening to a bunch of others share their similar traumas. It felt like I was living through theirs, too—adding more trauma to the pile already in my head. So, I didn't want to open up to people.

At the same time, I didn't have a partner I could talk to. Even before the divorce, I had tried to say that I felt like I was struggling. But I was sleeping on the couch. We weren't intimate. There was nothing left between us. I also felt there was a lot of distrust, a lot going on behind my back. Maybe that was the PTSD talking—or maybe it was that second voice in my head saying, *She's not being faithful, and she's not being kind to your kids.* Whatever the case, the PTSD made me stop being the happy-go-lucky guy I used to be.

As you've seen throughout this book, I'm someone who wants to move forward, who believes I can get through things—that I am enough. But once I realized I needed to do this for *me*—not to prove anything to anyone else—and that loving yourself comes first, I struggled. And that's when I started using alcohol to numb everything, to cover it up. It's unfortunate that I drank and made some of the choices I did. I was never mean to my children—but during that time, I wasn't making good choices.

I thought my then-soon-to-be ex was still helping take care of the kids. But instead, she was tearing me down, telling me I was just being weak. Regardless, returning home from war and managing post-traumatic stress disorder was a challenge.

I chose to fight. I fought against the urge to give up, to crawl into a shell, and stop functioning. I refused stem blocks or nerve blockers to numb the pain. Instead, I chose to dig deep into myself. Through it all, I stayed strong and kept making the best choices I could—choices that, at the beginning, felt impossible. I was walking away from a broken marriage, struggling with the idea of medically retiring from the military, and trying to figure out what was next.

After a horrible divorce, I was left asking myself: *Do I really want to find my forever person, or am I done altogether? Should I just be a single dad?* All of these questions weighed heavily on me. And while I was trying to do what was best for myself, I have to admit, there were times when I wasn't mentally there for my children. When they truly needed me—emotionally—Dad wasn't present. Sure, I played Spider-Man with my son when he was little. We built with LEGOs. We raced toy cars. I played Barbies and Bratz with my daughter. We had tea parties. I read them bedtime stories. But as they got older and became more independent, I started stepping back, letting them be on their own. And I wasn't always there in the ways they needed. I've apologized for that.

To get to this level of awareness and healing, I had to dig deep. And I would encourage anyone—if you're struggling with PTSD, depression, or anything else—please talk to someone. Find somebody you trust. You don't have to look far. I can tell you this: the person who is there when you're crying will mean more than the hundreds who show up when you're laughing. Pay attention to the people who support you when you're at your weakest. If therapy doesn't feel right for you, talk to someone you believe in. For me, I always had my mom. Whether she wanted her son calling drunk and crying or not—I had her. And I'm thankful for that.

There were times I hit a very low place. Did I ever think about killing myself? No. But did I question my worth on this planet? Absolutely. Over and over again. Much of that stemmed from combat and everything that followed. I'd ask myself: *Was my mission really worth all this? Look at the life I came back to—another failed marriage. I'm grateful to be a single father, but here I am, trying to figure out my own mental struggles while trying to give my children the life they deserve.*

One of my best coping tools has always been staying active. I still go to the gym seven days a week—rain or shine, it doesn't matter. I train every day because that's where *I* get to decide how hard I push, how heavy I lift, what I work on, and how much time I give to myself. When the headphones go in, it's all about me—and no one else. That's how I start my day: with physical activity that clears my mind and gets me centered. I also practice meditation and positive self-talk—projecting helpful thoughts or affirmations into the world. I do yoga. I meditate. I do all kinds of things to bring peace to my state of mind. Meditation doesn't mean you control your thoughts. Let your thoughts flow freely. But when one in particular comes up, find the one that brings peace. Truly, our minds are the only place we have to live—so why not make it an oasis? Stop making it a battle zone.

Build a strong support system around you. Connect with fellow veterans, support groups, your community, or trusted individuals—anyone who can offer understanding and help you feel less isolated. Isolation is one of the worst things you can do to yourself. Sitting in a corner and dwelling only makes things worse. As they say, "idle minds create chaos." It's hard to control the monster in your head when you're stuck replaying all the *would've, should've, could've* thoughts. Be grateful that you're alive to start another day.

Consider whether a service animal could help you. For me, a service animal didn't work because, at the time, I didn't want any public attention. I just wanted to be invisible—to go shopping like a ghost, in and out unnoticed. A dog only drew attention I wasn't ready for. But hey, if it helps you, go for it. Service animals and emotional support animals can be life-changing. They can assist with daily tasks and help you feel more connected to society. Like I said, build coping mechanisms that work for *you*.

For me, that meant focusing on fitness and health. I focused on being a positive example to my children, on moving forward, and on reminding myself that I *can* accomplish anything—because I've been through it. I have the T-shirts from the trials I've survived. But instead of looking back at those experiences as purely painful, I try to see them as lessons learned. You've already lived through those hard chapters—now look at them not with shame, but as the reason you've grown into who you are today. If you look back and feel shame, it's probably because you're not that person anymore. And that's something to be proud of. Keep moving forward. You are enough.

One of the best things you can do is try to understand where your anxiety, depression, or PTSD is coming from. Call it what you want—but don't walk around saying, "I have PTSD." Your mind is powerful. If you focus on healing and growth, you can transform your internal dialogue and your identity. As I like to say, "Speaking words is casting spells"—you're forecasting reality. Say, "I can." Say, "I will." Don't say, "I have PTSD," or "I'm an alcoholic." Instead, say, "I don't do that anymore." Say, "I've recovered from that." Everything must move in a positive, forward direction. We often trap ourselves with limiting language: "I am this" or "I have that." No—you don't. You can break free of those chains. But you have to believe that you are enough. Remember, recovery is your journey.

And, as I've said throughout this book, it's essential to find strategies and support systems that resonate with you. Seeking professional help and surrounding yourself with people who care can make a huge difference in reclaiming control over your mental health. It took me a long time to find the right person—and the right therapist—to talk to. But it was worth it. You might have to shop around for the right person, but I believe it's always better to have somebody to talk to. I don't want to burden the people I cherish most with everything I've gone through in my life, because many of us are people-pleasers. We like making others happy. And when we share trauma with someone we care deeply about, they often feel compelled to try to fix it.

So they end up taking on our burdens. I'm not looking for people to fix me. I love that people care for me and appreciate me, but I don't need to place the responsibility of my emotional healing on their shoulders. We are responsible for our own thoughts and feelings. You *do* have the power to control your mind.

As I keep saying, it starts with finding the positive in everything. You're not a victim—you're a survivor. Instead of saying, "I can't do that," or "I don't know how," say, "I haven't learned that yet." Be open to learning, but stop speaking in the negative. Believe in yourself. Your mind—your belief in yourself—is the most powerful tool you have on this planet.

Just remember: whether it's a lesson or a blessing, there is always something good that comes from every experience. And I know this might sound crazy, but I promise you: once I embraced that belief, it led me down the most amazing spiritual path. It gave me freedom. It helped me free my mind and discover the power we all have when we truly believe in ourselves.

At the end of the day, what matters most to me is being able to look in the mirror at night, give myself a high five, and say: *You kicked butt today. You did it.* Even if it was just waking up and getting myself out of bed—that counts. Because there are days when I fall into a dark hole. I struggle. I make it to the gym, but I'm not into it. It doesn't lift me out of the funk.

But I keep reminding myself: *Thank God, I'm still alive. Thank God for one more day. And may I please have one more try tomorrow?* That's all we can really hope for. If you're struggling, focus on one task at a time. But get outside. Take a walk. Staying in that dark place only pulls you deeper down.

As I've said in earlier chapters: No one should ever take their life. Your life is precious, and you belong here. Whether you're making good choices or not-so-great ones right now, you can change your path. No matter where you are in life, no matter what you've been through—trauma, mistakes, losses—you have the ability to choose what happens next. What defines your character is not what happened to you, but the choices you make afterward. Those choices will strengthen you and shape you into someone you never thought you could become. All it takes is truly believing that you are enough.

Chapter 10 Challenge: Elevate Your Circle

Surround yourself with people who uplift and challenge you—for one week. Intentionally connect with positive, like-minded individuals. Whether you journal your experience or reflect on it in your own way, take that week and look back. See how much it shifts your perception—of life, of yourself, of everything around you. Because the truth is: we don't have to live in a doom-and-gloom state.

Another thing I'd love to share with my readers is how to achieve real healing and growth. Truly, you have to find your *why*, and you have to believe that you're not broken. You have to believe that your struggles don't make you weak—regardless of whether you're a man or a woman. In our society, facing mental struggles is often seen as a sign of weakness. And for a long time, I saw it that way too. But I eventually realized that my mental health challenges were blocking me from living a good life—from truly enjoying quality time with my children, from communicating well with family, from being open to meeting new people, and from doing anything beyond just going to work and coming home. That was it.

I wasn't really living. In every other part of life, I just wasn't functioning like myself. I was trying to get back to being the happy-go-lucky guy I used to be—one of the kindest, gentlest teddy bears you'd ever meet. Sure, I might look like I could destroy things, but the last thing I ever wanted to harm was another human being.

And that's when I had to dig deep and realize that this doesn't make me weak. It doesn't make me broken. It doesn't make me less of a human being. It simply means I've faced things that many people would have fallen apart under—or curled up in a ball and cried through. No matter what challenge you've faced, you need to recognize that you survived something others can't even imagine. And that survival means you're strong enough to get help—to lift that weight off your shoulders.

You can overcome this. You can do it without medication, if that's your choice. You can do it through natural means. Even nutrition can help improve depression. But the first step is discovering that power within you—the power to say: *It's okay to be a man and cry. It's okay to be a man and feel lost. It's okay to be a woman and not have it all together.* It doesn't matter who you are. You don't have to have it all figured out. We are here on this planet to learn. And part of learning is going through struggles.

Part of those struggles is pain—and that pain needs to be spoken about, shared. You need to find a space where you feel safe sharing it. And if you don't feel safe sharing within your relationship, I would encourage you to reconsider that relationship. Because if your partner can't support you through your mental health journey, are they really your partner? Are they really part of your team? Find someone who will be there when you're crying—someone who will lift you up. And if that person isn't in your life yet, talk to a therapist.

Either way, please know: it does not make you weak. You are enough. And you need to believe that. That belief can truly change your life. That's what I had to determine for myself. Do I want to move forward, or do I want to lay on the couch, cry about my pain and suffering, and expect people to just leave me alone because I served my country and "deserve" to be left alone? If I had chosen that path, I wouldn't be here writing this book. But I'm here—because I want to remind you that it's okay.

We can heal from this. But you have to remember: it starts with you. We don't have to believe we're stuck with the things we struggle with. If we can overcome them, we no longer have them. We can be healed. Therapy is just one part of the process—believing in yourself and knowing you're enough is another. It is vital to know that you have value just by breathing air. Your strength comes from being challenged. We must fight our own fears, rise to meet those challenges head-on, and take the lead in our own lives. No one else can get you where you want to be. You have to be the one who gets up every day, grateful for another opportunity to move forward—in whatever way you choose. I believe in lessons and blessings in life. No matter how your day goes, there's always something to learn. It all depends on how you look at the challenge —or the lesson.

11

SINGLE FATHERHOOD
AND HEALTH CRISIS

A s I was transitioning out of the military, and dealing with my mental health struggles, I picked up an environmental job thanks to my background in chemical, biological, and nuclear fields. That made me a specialist in areas such as asthma safety and confined space rescue. So, while going through my medical retirement, I landed a solid civilian job. The company even agreed to fly me back and forth from Oregon to home once a month so I could check in with my unit while my medical review board process was still ongoing.

In essence, I was almost double-dipping—I used my paid leave to work the new job while wrapping up my military responsibilities. I took a position as the operations manager for this environmental company, and they sent me to Oregon to mentor a struggling project manager who was overseeing a Department of Energy job. The project involved a power conversion station that converts AC power to DC before sending it down transmission lines to California. DC power is more efficient for long-distance transmission because it's more stable.

I'm no electrician, but I understood enough to know why this work mattered. When word got out that I was coming to mentor this manager, I learned the company was on the verge of losing a $15 million contract. Meanwhile, I was exiting the military, transitioning into single fatherhood, and figuring out part-time custody for my kids. If I had to travel, they'd stay with my mom and dad. That part was tough—I'd already spent so much time away from them due to military service. Still, the company put me up in a nice suite in Oregon because of my role. I felt guilty about that.

Once I moved up there, I hired a nanny and had my kids living with me in the suite. Meanwhile, the rest of the team stayed in small, standard hotel rooms. That bothered me. I'm the kind of person who believes in equality—I don't see myself as better than anyone. If I were still in the military, I'd be down in the dirt with my soldiers. That's just how I've always led—by example, and with humility. I'm happy to share what I've learned, and I love telling these stories—because they show what I've been able to overcome in life. Long story short (funny thing to say in a book, I know), we ended up living in that hotel room. I was flying back and forth for my medical reviews. The nanny would take my kids around, showing them beautiful Oregon.

I tried the dating scene a bit—enough to realize it sucked. I did my best. I was doing P90X in the hotel room, trying to stay healthy and keep my mind sharp. The suite had a little stovetop, so I could cook. It was small, but functional. It was our home base during that strange but important transition in my life. So I was cooking meals, taking care of things, doing it all.

When I first got up there, I had to take over this project. I ended up sitting down with the team and discovering something important. When I first arrived, they were being micromanaged to the bone. The project was six months behind schedule, over a million dollars over budget, and on the verge of having the contract pulled. So I sat down with every single employee to understand how things had gotten to that point. All these employees wanted—something many of you probably want from your own leaders—was: "Treat me like the person you hired. Treat me with respect. Believe I'm capable. Include me. Make me feel like part of the team. Let me have a voice."

This was a government contract to clean up mercury and asbestos at a facility, and the team had lost all sense of direction. They had no goals—nothing to look forward to. They didn't know what was coming next. So I started doing what I had done in the military: communicating clear short-term and long-term goals. The same kind of goals we set for ourselves. With this structure in place, I was able to show them the path forward. We turned the entire project around. Not only did we catch up, but the team was awarded additional work at the same facility. But behind the scenes, I was still trying to figure out my own life—single fatherhood, career transition, lingering mental health struggles, and the question of whether I even wanted to try for a new relationship.

And then, five or six months into the contract, everything changed. I was taking a shower one morning. I bent over—just to pull up my underwear—and suddenly, I felt *flames* shoot down my legs. Just like that, I couldn't feel them anymore. Thank goodness I managed to get my underwear up, but after that, I couldn't stand. My fourteen-year-old son—my middle child, who was living there with my youngest daughter and me—had to come help. It took him over an hour to help me slide from the bathroom to the couch. But in that moment, I wasn't panicking about my legs. What hurt me more was the burden I felt I was placing on my son—making him help me like that. I could still feel pressure and weight, but my ability to walk was just gone.

After I made it to the couch, my son ran down the hallway to get help from my crew. And because of the rapport and respect I had built with them, I truly believe they responded like my soldiers would. They jumped into action. They rented a wheelchair, helped lift me into it, loaded me into the company van, and took me to the hospital.

I was put on bed rest for four days. My son had to help me with everything—getting around, getting through each day. I went from being an active guy who worked out regularly, raising his kids, rebuilding a career after military life, still wrestling with mental health, and figuring out the next chapter, to suddenly being in a wheelchair.

But even that didn't stop me. My crew built a wheelchair ramp for me, and I kept going. I was still able to function, still able to lead. Thankfully, I was only in the wheelchair for about sixty-five days. But during that time, I unknowingly pushed myself into a deeper health crisis.

I went from cooking meals, exercising, staying active, and moving around—to ordering fast food and living a more sedentary life. I could no longer cook for myself, let alone for my children. I was isolated, confined to a wheelchair, and overwhelmed. During this period—during what I felt was my weakest moment—I gained ninety-eight pounds. I went from being a 190-pound lean, mean, war-fighting machine to nearly 300 pounds, wearing a size forty-six, walking with a cane. I looked like seventy-seven percent of other

Americans on the verge of chronic illness. And that's when I met my wife. I was at my absolute lowest.

Of course, to this day, she still laughs and says I "catfished" her on the dating app—because the photos I used were from when I was still fit. I honestly didn't realize just how much weight I had put on. I had told her during our chats that I'd gained some weight and was aware of it, but man... I really didn't know the extent of it until I saw photos of myself later.

Meeting her was the first step. I was still working on the project up in Oregon, and I flew her up a couple of times. We had a few great trips, and our relationship grew. As you can probably tell, we ultimately got married. Through her, I discovered a chiropractor who specializes in muscle reactivation therapy.

Now, I'm the kind of person who avoids pills and pharmaceuticals. I've always leaned toward natural healing. I don't even take ibuprofen or use other nonorganic methods to heal. I believe the body can heal itself, and maybe that belief has been a blessing in disguise. Through muscle reactivation therapy, I learned that I had six muscles that had been shut off for nearly thirteen years—ever since my injury in Iraq.

The steroid epidurals I'd been given were just Band-Aids, masking the real issues. If I had gotten muscle reactivation therapy earlier to wake up my glutes, lower back, parts of my lats, and my hamstrings, my body would have supported itself properly. That support would have reduced pressure on my spine and allowed the damaged discs to begin healing naturally. Avoiding inflammatory foods would have helped, too. Still, even in this deeply vulnerable state, I managed to find light and begin to recover. Plus, this journey was being supported by my new girlfriend and future wife, who you will learn much more about in Chapter 12.

The muscle reactivation was just the beginning of my true healing journey. From there, I started exploring my overall health. My doctor kept telling me I was "healthy," but something still didn't feel right. My wife and I began experimenting with different diets—Mediterranean, this one, that one. We paid a personal trainer for over three years, which we felt helped with accountability. But it wasn't until I gained true knowledge of true whole-body nutrition down to our microbiota that everything changed. Whole-body nutrition is where it started—and that's ultimately what transformed my life. So I want to remind all of my readers: Never give up on yourself. Never let doubt, darkness, or what I like to call *the green monster,* take control of your thoughts.

Whether you're in a wheelchair, just went through a breakup, or feel abandoned—remember: maybe that person leaving you was a blessing. Maybe you didn't need them anyway. No matter what you're facing, I'm not sharing my story about rising from a wheelchair to say I'm better than anyone. I'm sharing it to say this: We all have it within us.

It's truly about saying, "I'm not going to give up—ever." Granted, if the feeling hadn't eventually come back to my legs, I would've had to learn to walk with braces or some other kind of support. But I would've found a way to stay upright and keep moving forward.

The last thing I wanted was to spend my life sitting still, being wheeled around, or being treated differently because I was in a wheelchair. And the truth is, no one with special needs wants to be treated differently. They just want to be treated like everyone else. If someone with special needs needs help, they'll ask for it. This is not to say that you should feel ashamed to offer help either—most people appreciate the gesture. But sometimes people want to struggle through it themselves, to prove that they can. You're not a bad person whether you offer or don't offer help. What matters most is believing that you have the ability to overcome anything.

As I always say: we are all unique human beings. We shouldn't put a ceiling on our potential. We must remember—we can reach the stars if we truly believe. We can do anything. Our minds are incredibly powerful. But we've got to break free of the chains we put on ourselves. No matter the burden on your shoulders, if you love yourself, believe in yourself, and remember that we were created with the power to heal—emotionally, spiritually, and even physically—you can begin to move forward. Healing begins with love—loving yourself, truly and fully. I choose to never give up.

I choose to keep moving forward, to focus on the present, to face challenges head-on. I know I am enough, and I can accomplish anything I focus my energy on. We all have this ability. The real question is: *How hard are you willing to push yourself?* Consider Michael Jordan. People don't talk about the 9,000 shots he *missed*— they talk about the game-winners and the championships. Look at anyone successful. They're remembered for the few moments of glory. But if you don't look at the daily work they put in behind the scenes, you're fooling yourself. Nothing comes easy—not for anyone. Whatever your goal is in life, pursue it with intention, energy, and focus. If you only give fifty percent, you'll only get fifty percent back. Don't kid yourself into thinking life is just going to hand you success.

Your experiences are yours. They're shaped by your choices and how much effort you're willing to put into the life you want to live. For me, I'm more inspired now than ever. I want to live my life, to explore it, to stay focused on positivity, and to continue building connections with my adult children, my grandchildren, and my own spiritual path. That's what has lifted me up. And now, I want to give back—to remind you that you are enough.

Chapter 11 Challenge: The Resilience Challenge

Identify one setback from your past, and journal how it shaped you. Then write down how you will use that lesson to push yourself forward in your current journey. As you reflect on that setback, don't see it as a failure—see it as a turning point. That moment helped *shape* you. Use it. Whether it's something you couldn't let go of, the "wheelchair" you're trying to rise from, the "ball and chain" holding you back—whatever it is, it doesn't define you. Use it as fuel. Let it empower you. Then move forward.

_____

_____

_____

_____

NEW MARRIAGE AND THE JOURNEY TO HOLISTIC HEALTH

S o, you've probably figured out that I ultimately ended up marrying my best friend and wife after dating for eleven months. When I came home from the project in Oregon, it became clear—we were deeply bonded. I lived on one side of town, she lived on the other, but we knew we wanted to be together. We both knew what we wanted—and, just as importantly, what we no longer wanted in our lives.

My wife, being the amazing woman she is, suggested something pretty unique for our honeymoon: we went to a firearms training facility and completed four days of concealed carry training. We told our family they could meet us at the White Wedding Chapel in Las Vegas. We'd both been through the big wedding thing before, and we weren't interested in spending a bunch of money or energy on a show. We knew we wanted to spend our lives together—no whoop-dee-do necessary. Right from the start, I thought: *Wow, is this too good to be true?*

Another beautiful part of this journey was becoming a stepfather to three incredible children. Tragically, when I first began dating their mother, the children had lost their father—he had taken his own life. That's one of the reasons I'm so passionate about advocating for mental health, self-worth, and believing that we are enough. Everything happens for a reason, and I've done my best to be there for those kids in the only way I know how. But blending families is no easy task—especially when both of you are bringing teenage children into a new relationship.

My own children had already endured a horrible stepmother. They eventually told me about the abuse they suffered at her hands when I wasn't there. They were too scared to speak up at the time, afraid of the consequences. We never expect our partners to be capable of that kind of harm. I knew my ex-wife could be narcissistic and selfish, but I believed she was at least treating my children well. Sadly, that wasn't the case. So, understandably, my kids weren't sure they were ready to accept a new stepmother in their lives—especially after finally getting some one-on-one time with me.

For a while, they felt like they had Disneyland Dad all to themselves. With a nanny and the freedom to explore Oregon, things were amazing. Life finally felt fun, safe, and centered around them. I hope they understand now that when you find the person who lifts you up—and you know, deep in your soul, that they are the one—you hold on to that.

This relationship has been like nothing I've ever experienced. I found a woman who truly wants the best for me and for my children—unconditionally. It took the challenges of my past to teach me what I was really looking for in life. Through those hard-earned lessons, I discovered what I wanted, what I was willing to accept, and what I needed for my health and well-being. Unbeknownst to both of us, we were survivors of difficult pasts. My wife had endured eighteen years in an abusive marriage. The trauma she experienced was deep, but so was her strength. Together, we embraced the challenge of blending our families—bringing her three children and my three children together. My oldest son never lived with us full-time, but still, we became a version of the Brady Bunch: three boys, three girls, a couple of dogs... just minus Alice.

I'd always wanted a big family, but I had no idea how many challenges, perceptions, and emotional hurdles would come with trying to blend our two families together. Some of the children resented what had happened. Some felt neglected or unheard. And looking back now, I can see areas where we could have done better. That's part of being human—not dwelling in guilt, but reflecting on what went wrong, what went right, and then making changes to prevent the same mistakes in the future. It takes digging deep inside yourself, owning your part, and taking real action to create lasting change.

At the time my wife and I met, we were both drinking. But over time, my drinking got worse. I didn't even realize it at first. My wife thought she was doing something fun and thoughtful when she bought me a home beer-making kit. But, long story short, that led to way too much beer and way too much drinking—resulting in poor choices or, worse, a lack of choices altogether.

Things happen in life. And thank goodness my wife is the loving, caring woman she is. She recognized that my drinking and behavior were symptoms of unhealed mental struggles—challenges I had faced but never fully processed. She stuck by me, and eventually, it led to a turning point: I gave up alcohol, began making better choices, and started seeing my past in a new light. I was finally able to face the old demons and say: "I don't need this pain anymore. I don't need to keep talking about it, blaming others, or blaming situations for how I reacted." My reactions weren't because of my present—they were echoes of my past. But just because my old relationships were dysfunctional doesn't mean my current one has to be.

My wife is not my past. She is not the person who hurt me. Still, our subconscious minds like to store pain and treat it like a familiar warning. Whether or not the situation is actually the same, our subconscious interprets it that way. It's a trap: we're in healthy relationships, but we can't feel free or safe enough to open up, even though the circumstances are entirely different. Sometimes it's not just the past—it's how we present ourselves that affects whether we feel safe enough to be vulnerable.

Thankfully, I found a woman who embraces me, who understands me. She knows I live with PTSD. She knows there are struggles we'll face. And often, she's set herself aside to help carry me through hard moments. In return, I've made it my mission to lift her up in her life, her career, and her dreams. But through all of this, I know I've caused pain. My actions—or lack of action—have hurt the children. I've chosen to apologize to them with an open heart and a clear mind. I know I'm far from perfect—none of us are. We're here to learn and grow in a positive direction. What it ultimately came down to was feeling safe enough and strong enough to cry in front of my wife. To express my emotions without shouting, blaming, or hiding behind anger. That took courage. And it took acknowledging that I still needed more mental health therapy.

I fought a battle with my combat experiences. I looked back at all of it—every mission—and understood that there was a purpose. I followed orders. I focused on the humanitarian efforts to help me process it all: handing out school supplies to children, playing soccer with young people, showing those we were trying to liberate from terrorist regimes that we were kind, compassionate people—not just warriors, not just soldiers with a thirst for battle. We were humans first, and we showed that through acts of kindness.

Now, I can tell you this: special operators are capable of the most incredible missions. We are highly motivated and exceptionally trained. But the truth is—we are also some of the most caring humans when it comes to giving back to our brothers and sisters. Because that's what we all are: brothers and sisters. And we need to support one another instead of tearing each other down. I don't focus on the targets that were destroyed or the missions completed. I focus on the good that happened. I survived everything else.

My wife has taught me a lot—reminding me that I am a survivor. That I am enough. That I can keep going. Eventually, I sought out an incredible counseling center here called Meadow-brook Counseling. It's owned by someone who truly cares about treating people holistically. They don't push medication. They don't make you feel unsafe or unheard. There, I found an amazing therapist. I finally started to share my story and began healing.

My wife and I had an incredible relationship, but we were still having our battles. I realized there was more work I needed to do on myself. Because I had found my person, my rock—and I wasn't going to let my unhealed struggles bounce off of her and push her away, or damage the family I love more deeply than any relationship I've ever been in.

This relationship made me feel safe. It made me feel free, loved, cared for, and trusted. So, I decided it was time—really time—to go back into therapy. Through that process, I experienced *ketamine therapy*. I had a full body scan at a holistic wellness center and discovered that I had damage to my frontal lobe. Ketamine, used in controlled therapy, helps regrow neural connections. They call it fertilizer for the brain.

When we experience trauma, our neural pathways can fray, break, or get rerouted in unhealthy ways. We end up defaulting to fight-or-flight over and over because it's the only well-worn path left in our minds. Without rebuilding those other neural networks, we lose the ability to pause, process, and understand our emotions before reacting. That ability—to say, *Where is this feeling coming from? Why do I feel this way? What triggered it?*—is so important.

Trust me, I struggled. And sometimes, the way I expressed my feelings made others feel like I was blaming them, even when that wasn't my intent. I never wanted to hurt people or place blame. I've always been someone who owns my mistakes. If I've dug myself into a hole, I'll be the one to climb out. That mindset has made leadership hard at times. I've often wanted to do everything myself, because I knew I'd do it right. But how can you empower talented people—people you trust—if you never let them prove themselves?

Therapy, and especially ketamine therapy, changed my life. It helped me see things more clearly. I was able to realize that reconnecting neural pathways in my frontal lobe—without relying on prescription drugs—was possible. Through six therapy sessions and carefully guided ketamine treatment, I focused deeply on healing my mind. And I want to share something powerful with you all: during that time, I spoke to God. He surrounded me with light and told me that everything I had been through—everything I had endured—was because I am a strong soul, and I'm here for a purpose. That purpose is to push forward, to promote wellness, and to teach others that we are enough and that we can keep going forward.

Following this path of holistic health and truly understanding how my body works is what helped me rise. I went from being nearly 300 pounds (wearing a size forty-six and walking with a cane, as I mentioned earlier) when I first met my wife, to becoming a man who competed in the Mr. Health & Fitness competition with *Muscle & Fitness* magazine—at 5.3 percent body fat. That transformation was not from shortcuts, pills, or quick fixes. It was from learning and practicing holistic health and wellness. But in order to open my mind, I had to empty my cup completely. I had to let go of everything I thought I knew—because not everything is as it seems.

Now, I'm not ending this book to convince you I'm a conspiracy theorist. But I do want to say this clearly: true health begins with whole-body wellness and nutrition. I walked away from my position as a government-appointed director to teach holistic health and wellness full-time—because I had seen firsthand what it could do. I had seen how it could free the mind from depression.

Did you know that over eighty percent of your serotonin is produced in your intestines, and around fifty percent of your dopamine is stored in the walls of your stomach? Your body is filled with microorganisms that regulate your health. You have to feed yourself at the cellular level. When you take in chemicals, synthetics, hybrid foods, or GMO products, your liver doesn't know how to process them. It stores them in fat—because your body is smart, and it's trying to protect you. That fat often gathers around your belly, legs, neck, and even your head—but not so much around your heart. Your body's goal is survival, even if it means sacrificing your optimal function.

Today's diet—loaded with ultra-processed and toxin-filled foods —is harming us. I learned this the hard way. Even with personal trainers, I wasn't being taught real nutrition. I was taught about macro diets and general plans, but none of it addressed what truly mattered: identifying non-inflammatory, whole foods and buying organic. Choosing clean, nutrient-dense products and feeding the body intentionally. We're all different and unique, and that means our health journeys will be, too. This understanding led me to start my own business: All In Forward Health and Wellness. Since then, I've become a certified nutritionist, a nationally certified health and wellness coach, a certified personal trainer, and a certified transformation specialist.

I'm currently pursuing my second master's degree—this time in Clinical Nutrition—because I believe that if you don't seek the truth through learning for yourself, you'll never break free from the pack. You'll stay lost. But if you're willing to rise, to learn, and to walk your own path—especially a spiritual one—you will find your way, just as I did.

And yes, having an amazing partner by my side who supports me has helped me immensely. Her love and encouragement continue to be a powerful source of strength. I mean, she joined the same journey. She, too, went from wearing a size 10–12 to a size 2 just by changing her eating habits.

And she'll tell anyone: it's not about how she looks now—it's about how she feels. That's exactly what I want to share with my readers.

I hope this journey, as a whole, inspires and empowers you to find yourself, recognize your triumphs, reframe your past as lessons and blessings, and simply be grateful to be alive. Whether you're spiritual or not, know that there is something bigger than yourself.

Be at peace with who you are. Because selfless service—giving back to others—is one thing I will always do. Yes, it makes me feel good. I'll admit that. But that's not a bad thing. Helping others lifts my spirit, and I will always extend a hand to those in need. That's just who I am. I encourage every one of us to find our own spiritual path. Find your happiness. Find your place. And once you do, use that power to uplift your community. To help others. To inspire. To leave this world better than it was when you arrived. We're not here to fix everything or make life easy for everyone. We're here to help. To lift others. To inspire. Because the easy road often leads to emptiness. True fulfillment comes from challenges—challenges that teach us new skills, build our character, and bring light into our lives.

But I can't stress this enough: sometimes, in order to rebuild, you have to empty your cup. I've shed a cocoon in this new phase of life. I had to let go of being a soldier, of being rigid and closed off. I had to return to who I *really* am—a compassionate, loving, happy-go-lucky person. That return to self came through two things: laying it all out in therapy, and discovering holistic health. Feeding my body with the right nutrients gave me what I needed to feel joy again. To balance my hormones naturally. To heal.

Getting regular physical exercise has helped keep me on track, too. Many people don't even know that walking just 150 minutes a week can add seven years to your life. That's just ten minutes after every meal—and it even helps stabilize blood sugar. But this kind of knowledge isn't widely taught. It's unfortunate that people have to seek out voices like mine just to learn what this earth already provides to keep us healthy, thriving, and resilient. Our bodies have the power to fight off disease, even cancer—but it all depends on what we feed them. The same goes for your life. Whatever effort you put in is exactly what you'll get in return.

So I ask you: How do you want to be remembered? Do you want to leave a legacy? Or do you want to be one of those nameless stones in the grass—someone people pass by and say, "Oh, this person died forty years ago," without ever knowing who you truly were? I don't care if my name ends up written on a wall somewhere. All I hope is that by sharing my life, my struggles, and the challenges I still face every day, you realize that you can make it too. You, too, can start a business. You can go back to college. You can rebuild relationships with family members you've lost. You can open your mind to learning new things. You can take a walk every day—just ten minutes after each meal—for your health.

You can make these choices. It's about choosing your "hard" and choosing to overcome. That decision must be made at the end of every challenge. Don't wallow. Don't blame others for where you are. Yes, people may have hurt you. They may have caused pain or setbacks. But if you stay in that place—if you keep blaming them— you're just drinking poison, hoping the other person gets sick. You stay stuck. You stop moving forward.

Look at life through the windshield, not the rearview mirror. The rearview mirror is small for a reason—it's not meant to be your focus. Keep your eyes on the road ahead. Hope for the best. Focus on the now. That's what I challenge you to do: Believe in yourself. Know that you are enough.

Find your purpose. Find your reason why—whether it's your children, your health, or simply the desire to live another day. Whatever it is, find it. With that purpose comes the strength to share your skills that you've worked hard to learn with others.

But always remember: you are enough just by breathing. Everything else—the talents, the skills, the service you offer—is a bonus. It's your gift to the world, but it does not define your worth. That's one of the greatest lessons I've learned through this entire journey. I have value. Sure, I didn't win Mr. Health and Fitness 2024. I finished in the top twenty out of twenty thousand people—and that's amazing. But more importantly: *I did it*. I faced my fear. Was I scared?

Absolutely. But fear is just that—fear. It's like being scared of an interview that hasn't happened yet, or dreading jumping out of an airplane before you even reach the door. Fear holds us back.

It's that child in the corner saying, "I don't dare." And sometimes we just need someone to take our hand, stand that child up, and say, "You've got this. You can do this." And from there—believe that you are enough. The path won't be easy. The brighter your light, the more shadows you'll cast. But ignore the shadows. Keep shining. Keep sharing your light with others, just as I've tried to share mine with you.

Chapter 12 Challenge: Try a Personal Development Challenge

For one week, read ten pages of an inspiring book or listen to a motivational podcast every day. Absorb new wisdom. Apply at least one key takeaway to your life. I suggest this because, yes, I hope this book has inspired you—but sometimes we need to keep feeding our minds with daily affirmations and reminders. Hearing stories from others who made it—who overcame—can spark something inside of us. It can remind you of this truth: You can do this. You are enough. And you are capable of amazing things.

FINAL THOUGHTS

I f there's one truth I hope you take from my story, it's this: **you are built for greatness.** You were not born to simply survive—you were born to rise, to overcome, to become everything you were created to be. No matter where you come from, no matter what you've faced, **you carry something powerful within you.** And that power? It's called *resilience.*

I shared these chapters of my life not to impress you—but to impress upon you that anything is possible when you refuse to quit. We all need reminders sometimes that **we are not alone**—and we're not meant to walk this path in isolation. Surround yourself with people who fuel your fire, not those who try to dim it. Build a tribe that speaks life into your vision and stands with you through the valleys and the victories.

At the end of the day, **you are enough.** Not once you hit a goal. Not once you lose the weight or get the job or earn the degree. **Right now. Just as you are.** But don't let that stop you from striving.

Growth is not about fixing what's broken—it's about uncovering the strength that's already inside you.

Life will throw obstacles your way—some big, some brutal. But hear me: **every obstacle is an opportunity that is wearing a disguise.** Every setback is setting you up for a greater comeback—*if* you choose to rise. And that's what this world needs—more people who choose to rise. More people who take that first scary step toward change. Go back to school. Start that business. Walk away from what no longer serves you. Bet on yourself, and keep showing up.

Every day is a blank canvas. Don't let fear be the brush that paints your future. Paint it with courage. Paint it with faith. Paint it with the boldness of someone who knows they still have a purpose to fulfill.

America still holds opportunity—but you've got to be willing to work, to believe, to keep pushing. Don't buy the lie that your background, your skin color, your past, or your pain defines your ceiling. That's a lie designed to keep you small—and you were never meant to play small.

The only real failure is quitting. As long as you're breathing, you're still in the fight. And when you reach the summit of one mountain, celebrate the view—but don't stop climbing. Because there's more in you. More hills. More victories. More growth. And every step forward is proof that you're still becoming the person you were called to be.

So breathe. Reconnect. Walk in nature. Listen to the stillness. Reflect on how far you've come. And then—**keep going.**

Thank you. Thank you for walking this journey with me. My hope is that something in these pages lit a fire inside you—a fire to break free, to grow stronger, to choose life more fully. I've dedicated myself to this path—not just for me, but for my wife, my children, and my grandchildren. I want to run with them in the backyard—not be bound by tubes or regret.

And if I can do it, **so can you.**

Now go show the world what you're made of.

THANK YOU FOR READING
MY BOOK!

To learn more about me and the businesses I'm passionate about, please scan the QR codes:

Slade Defense Women's Tactical Defense Training website

My business website for holistic health and wellness

Helping Heroes Heal is a non profit that provides mental health services for veterans, first responders, and their families. 100% of donations goes to the treatment.

I appreciate your interest in my book and value your feedback as it helps me improve future versions of this book. I would appreciate it if you could leave your invaluable review on Amazon.com with your feedback.
Thank you!

www.ingramcontent.com/pod-product-compliance
Lightning Source LLC
Chambersburg PA
CBHW021147090426
42740CB00008B/985